Oxford
KS3 Science

Activate

Question • Progress • Succeed

1

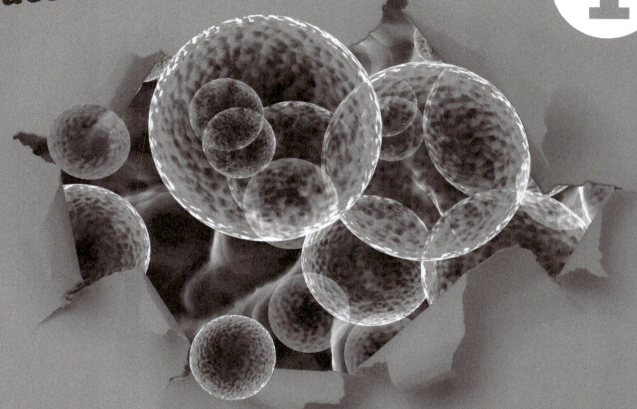

Workbook: Foundation
Including Diagnostic Pinchpoint activities

Jon Clarke
Philippa Gardom Hulme
Jo Locke

Assessment Editor
Dr Andrew Chandler-Grevatt

OXFORD
UNIVERSITY PRESS

Contents

Physics P1

Introduction

Welcome to your *Activate* 1 Workbook. This Workbook contains lots of practice questions and activities to help you to progress through the course.

Each chapter from the *Activate* 1 Student Book is covered and includes a summary of all the content you need to know. Answers to all of the questions are in the back of the Workbook so you will be able to see how well you have answered them.

Practice activities – Lots of questions and activities, increasing in difficulty, give you plenty of practice and help to build your confidence.

Hints – Helpful hints give you extra guidance on how to answer harder questions.

What you need to remember – At the end of each page, this box forms a summary of the key points you need to remember.

Revision questions – At the end of each of the Biology, Chemistry, and Physics sections you will find revision questions. These are exam-style questions to test your knowledge. They include a mix of short- and long-answer question types, as well as maths questions. Questions with one conical flask next to them are the easiest; questions with two flasks are harder.

Checklists – Revision checklists at the end of each section cover the content in the revision questions. You can tick the boxes to show how confident you feel with each area. The Maths icon shows that you will need to use your maths skills to answer the question.

Pinchpoints

A Pinchpoint is an idea or concept in science that can be challenging to learn. It is often difficult to say *why* these ideas are challenging to learn. The Pinchpoint intervention question at the end of each chapter focuses on a challenging idea from within the chapter. By answering the Pinchpoint question you will see whether you understand the concept or whether you have gone wrong. By doing the follow-up activity you will find out why you made the mistake and how to correct it.

Pinchpoint question – The Pinchpoint question is about a difficult concept from the chapter that students often get wrong. You should answer the Pinchpoint question and one follow-up activity. The Pinchpoint is multiple choice; answer the question by choosing a letter and then do the follow-up activity with the same letter.

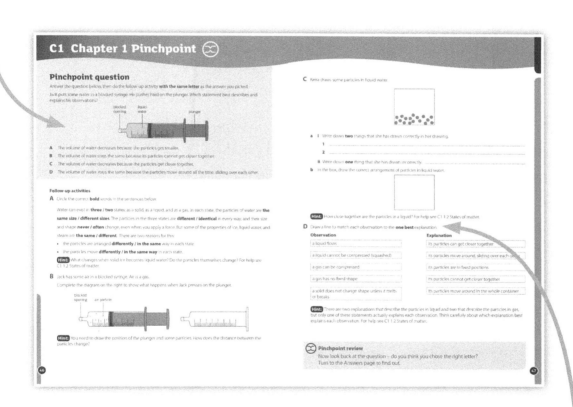

Pinchpoint follow-up – The follow-up activities will help you to better understand the difficult concept. If you got the Pinchpoint question right, the follow-up will develop your understanding further. If you got the Pinchpoint wrong, it will help you to see why you went wrong, and how to get it right next time.

WS1.1 Asking scientific questions
WS1.2 Planning investigations

A Draw a line to match each type of variable with its description.

independent	the variable that changes because of the variable you change
dependent	the variable you change
control	a variable that must be kept the same during an investigation

B Complete the table by ticking to show the type of data collected.

Data	✓ Continuous	✓ Discrete	✓ Categoric
eye colour			
hair length			
number of ladybirds			
temperature			
sex			
mass			

C For each of the following statements, circle the correct word in **bold**.

The measurements you collect in an investigation are called **variables / data**.

Accurate / precise data is close to the true value of what you are trying to measure.

Accurate / precise data has a very small spread when measurements are repeated.

Data is **repeatable / reproducible** if you repeat the investigation several times and get similar results.

Data is **repeatable / reproducible** if someone else repeats the investigation and gets similar results.

What you need to remember

The plan for an investigation starts with the scientific _____ you are trying to answer. You should make a _____ about what the answer might be, and use your scientific _____ to explain your prediction.

In your plan you should identify the _____ variable you will change, the _____ variable you will measure or observe, and a list of variables you will _____. Your plan should also include a list of the _____ you will use, and your method. You should also include a _____ _____ to make sure your investigation is as safe as possible.

The measurements or observations you make are called _____. It is important that they are accurate and _____. The investigations should be repeatable and _____.

WS1.3 Recording data

A A group of students carried out an investigation to measure how far a toy car travels down slopes of different steepness. The students measured:

- the angle of the ramp
- the total distance travelled by the car.

They took three repeat results for each angle, and then calculated a mean result.

Add headings to the table below to produce a results table for the students to collect their results.

B In the investigation in activity **A**, for a slope angle of 30° the students got the following distance readings:

60 cm   58 cm   80 cm

Circle the reading that is likely to be an **outlier**.

C Calculate the **mean** distance travelled from the data below and tick the correct answer.

Distance ball travelled (cm)	48	50	55

50 cm ☐   **7 cm** ☐

51 cm ☐   **45 cm** ☐

D For each of the following statements about graphs, circle the correct word in **bold**.

Plot the independent variable on the ***x-axis / y-axis***.

Plot the dependent variable on the ***x-axis / y-axis***.

Label the axis with the variable name and its **unit / symbol**.

If both the independent and dependent variables are continuous, you should plot a **bar chart / line graph**.

If your independent variable is categoric, you should plot a **bar chart / line graph**.

What you need to remember

Before starting an investigation you should produce a _____ table. You should put the

_____ variable in the first column, and allow space to take repeat _____ and calculate

a _____. Also remember to include _____ in the column headings. Check your data for

_____ – anomalous results, and _____ the measurement.

When plotting a graph, make sure you choose an appropriate _____ and put the independent

variable on the _____-axis. If both the dependent and independent variables are continuous, you

should plot a _____. If your independent variable is categoric you should plot a

_____. You can also display discrete or categoric data in a _____

_____.

WS1.4 Analysing data

A Define what is meant by a **line of best fit**.

_____

_____

B Plot the data from the table and draw a line of best fit.

Applied force (N)	Length of spring (mm)
5	13
10	22
15	26
20	35
25	46
30	52
35	59
40	64

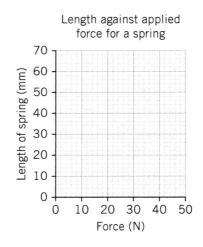

Length against applied force for a spring

C The data in activity **B** are from a student's experiment. The student predicted that as force got larger, the spring would be longer. Write a conclusion based on the data.

_____

_____

_____

_____

What you need to remember

It is often helpful to plot _____ from an experiment, and draw a line of _____

_____ in order to analyse the results. This might be a straight line or a _____, and goes

as near as possible to as many points as possible. A _____ will state what was found out and any

_____ found between the variables, and use _____ knowledge to explain the pattern

and compare the results with the _____.

WS1.5 Evaluating data

A Write **one** thing that you should include in an evaluation of an investigation.

_____

B A group investigates how bright a lamp is at different distances, using a light-sensitive meter.

A second group does a similar investigation.

When the two groups compare results they find differences in their data.

Suggest **two** reasons for these differences.

_____

_____

C Suggest **one** way that the groups in activity **B** can improve their investigation if they do it again.

_____

D Two different groups of students investigated the force exerted when a tennis ball is dropped from a height. The table shows their results.

| Group 1, force (N) | 12, 17, 14 |
| Group 2, force (N) | 12, 15, 14, 14, 13 |

a Which group should have more confidence in their results? _____

b Give a reason for your answer to part **a**.

_____

E For each type of error, suggest an example source and a way of reducing its effect.

a Random error

Example source _____

Way of reducing its effect _____

b Systematic error

Example source _____

Way of reducing its effect _____

What you need to remember

There are two ways to _____ your investigation. You should discuss the _____

of the _____ that you have collected, and suggest and explain _____ to your

_____ so you can collect data of better quality if you repeat the experiment. Your suggested

improvements should increase the _____ that you have in your conclusion. Having few, or no,

_____ in the data increases the confidence in the conclusion. The spread of data tells you how

_____ the data is. Having a small spread in the data will give you _____ confidence

in your conclusion. _____ errors, such as a digital mass balance only reading to the nearest 1 g,

can increase the spread, or cause outliers. _____ errors, such as a newtonmeter reading 1 N even

when there is nothing attached, can reduce the accuracy. You might get better data by including a bigger

_____ of the independent variable, or taking _____ readings.

Pinchpoint question

Answer the question below, then do the follow-up activity **with the same letter** as the answer you picked.

Linda and Samir are doing an investigation to find out how quickly sugar cubes dissolve at different temperatures.

Linda put one sugar cube in a beaker of water at 50 °C and stirred it at a steady speed. Samir timed how long it took the sugar cube to dissolve.

They then investigated how long it took the sugar cube to dissolve at temperatures of 60 °C and 70 °C, as shown in the diagram below.

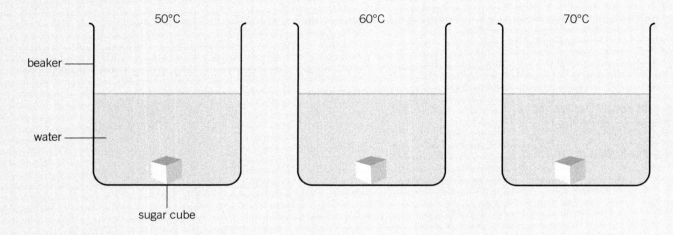

Circle the correct identification of the dependent, independent, and control variables for this investigation.

	dependent variable	independent variable	control variable
A	sugar cube	dissolving	stop watch
B	water temperature	time to dissolve	volume of water
C	time to dissolve	water temperature	stirring speed
D	time to dissolve	water temperature	dissolving

Follow-up activities

A Draw a line to link each type of variable to its definition and an example.

Type of variable	Definition	Example
dependent variable	the variable that you change	time to dissolve
independent variable	a variable that must be kept the same	water temperature
control variable	the variable that changes	stirring speed

Hint: What is the difference between the dependent, independent, and control variables? For help see WS 1.1 Asking scientific questions.

B **Underline** the dependent variable and **circle** the independent variable(s) in the following examples:

a Investigating the effect of the type of fertiliser on the height that sunflowers grow.

b How does the number of masses change the length of a spring?

c Investigating the time taken for an ice cube to melt at different temperatures.

d Investigating the temperature change of different coloured materials left in the sun.

e Comparing the time it takes tea to cool with milk, or without milk.

f Investigating the volume of water different brands of nappy can hold without leaking.

Hint: What is the difference between the dependent, independent, and control variables? For help see WS 1.1 Asking scientific questions.

C When carrying out the investigation, Linda and Samir need to control some variables.

Linda knew that she should control the **volume of water**, by measuring the same volume each time.

Samir knew that he should control the **size of the sugar cubes**, so he measured them to make sure each one was the same size.

a List some other variables that Linda and Samir will need to control.

_____

_____

_____

b Make a prediction for their investigation.

Hint: How should you form a prediction? For help see WS 1.1 Asking scientific questions.

_____

_____

c Give a scientific reason for your prediction.

_____

_____

D Tick the variables that Linda and Samir need to control in their investigation.

size of beaker ☐

volume of water in the beaker ☐

size of sugar cube ☐

type of sugar cube ☐

stirring speed ☐

water temperature ☐

person who uses timer ☐

room temperature ☐

Hint: What are control variables? For help see WS 1.1 Asking scientific questions.

Pinchpoint review

Now look back at the question – do you think you chose the right letter? Turn to the Answers page to find out.

B1.1 Observing cells

A Draw a line to match each sentence to its ending.

All living organisms are made up of	an organism.
Cells are the smallest units found in	cells.
Cells can only be seen through	a microscope.

B A light microscope is used to magnify objects.

Match each missing label on the diagram to the correct word below.
Write **W**, **X**, **Y**, or **Z** beside each word.

slide ☐   eyepiece lens ☐

objective lens ☐   light ☐

C The statements below can be reordered to explain how to use a light microscope to observe an object.
Read the statements and write down the order of statements that gives the best method.

Correct order ☐ ☐ ☐ ☐ ☐

1 Place the object you wish to observe on the stage.
2 Select the objective lens with the lowest magnification and look through the eyepiece.
3 Turn the fine focus knob until your object comes into focus.
4 Turn the coarse focus knob until you can see your object.
5 Move the stage to its lowest position.

What you need to remember

All living organisms are made up of _____ – these are the building blocks of life. To see cells in detail

you need to use a _____ . This _____ the object. Looking carefully and in detail at an

object is called making an _____ .

B1.2 Plant and animal cells

A Use the words in the box to label the main components of the animal and plant cells.

> **cell membrane**   **cell wall**   **chloroplast**   **cytoplasm**
> **mitochondrion**   **nucleus**   **vacuole**

Hint: Some words may need to be used more than once as they are found in both cells.

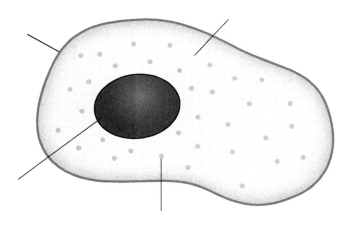 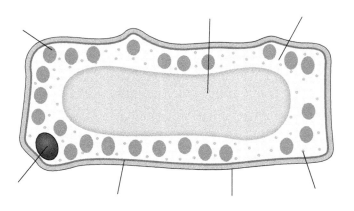

B Draw a line from each cell component to its function.

nucleus	contains cell sap to keep the cell firm
mitochondria	controls what comes in and out of a cell
chloroplast	where respiration occurs
vacuole	contains genetic material and controls the cell
cell membrane	where photosynthesis occurs

C List **two** similarities and **two** differences between plant and animal cells.

Similarities:

1 _____

2 _____

Differences:

1 _____

2 _____

What you need to remember

Plant and animal cells both contain a _____ that controls the cell, _____ where

chemical reactions take place, a _____ _____ that controls what comes in and out of

the cell and _____ where respiration occurs. Plant cells also contain a rigid _____

_____ that provides support, _____ for photosynthesis and a _____ that

contains cell sap to keep the cell firm.

B1.3 Specialised cells

A Many cells have special features to allow them to perform a particular function. These are called **specialised cells**.

Draw a line to match each specialised cell with its feature.

sperm cell	long and thin and transmits electrical impulses
nerve cell	contains lots of chloroplasts for photosynthesis
root hair cell	has a tail to swim
leaf cell	has a large surface area to absorb water

B Match the name of the specialised cell to its picture by writing the correct number in the box.

1

2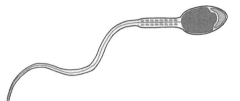

3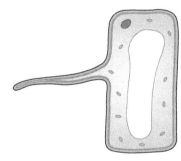

4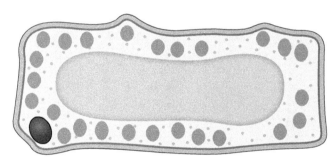

sperm cell   root hair cell

leaf cell    nerve cell

C Circle **true** or **false** for the following statements about red blood cells.

1	They carry oxygen around the body.	**true / false**
2	They have a nucleus.	**true / false**
3	They have a disc-like shape.	**true / false**
4	They have a large surface area.	**true / false**
5	They are found in plant cells.	**true / false**

What you need to remember

Some cells have special features to carry out their functions. These cells are called _____ cells. For example, in animals, _____ _____ cells have haemoglobin for carrying oxygen, and nerve cells are long and thin to carry electrical _____. _____ cells have a head and tail so they can carry male genetic material to the female egg. In plants, root _____ cells have a large surface area to absorb _____ and nutrients from the soil and leaf cells are packed with _____ to carry out photosynthesis.

B1.4 Movement of substances

A Many substances move into and out of your cells by diffusion.

Tick which of the following substances diffuse **into** your cells.

carbon dioxide ☐

oxygen ☐

glucose ☐

B Tick the **true** statements about diffusion.

1 Diffusion is the movement of particles from a place where they are in a low concentration to a place where they are in a high concentration. ☐

2 The higher the concentration, the more particles of a substance are present. ☐

3 Diffusion continues until there is the same concentration of the particles everywhere. ☐

C The diagrams below show diffusion taking place, but they are in the wrong order.

P   Q   R   S

Write the letters in the order that correctly shows diffusion. The first one has been done for you.

S ☐ ☐ ☐

D Circle the correct **bold** words in the sentences below to describe diffusion in plants.

Water molecules move from the soil where there is **high / low** water concentration into the **leaf / root** hair cells where there is **high / low** water concentration. Water then travels to other cells in the plant by diffusion.

Inside the cells, water fills up the **vacuole / cytoplasm** and makes the cell **floppy / rigid**. This helps the plant to stand upright. If the plant does not have enough water, the vacuole **shrinks / expands**. The cells then become **floppy / rigid** and the plant wilts.

What you need to remember

Substances move from an area where they are in a _____ concentration to an area where they are in

a _____ concentration. This process is called _____. Many substances move into and

out of your cells by using this process. For example in gas exchange, _____ diffuses into your cells

from the blood and _____ diffuses out of your cells into the blood, so that it can be taken to the

lungs and breathed out.

B1.5 Unicellular organisms

A Unicellular organisms are made up of just one cell.

Tick which **one** of the following is a unicellular organism.

cat ☐

daisy ☐

amoeba ☐

mushroom ☐

B This is a euglena. It lives in fresh water.

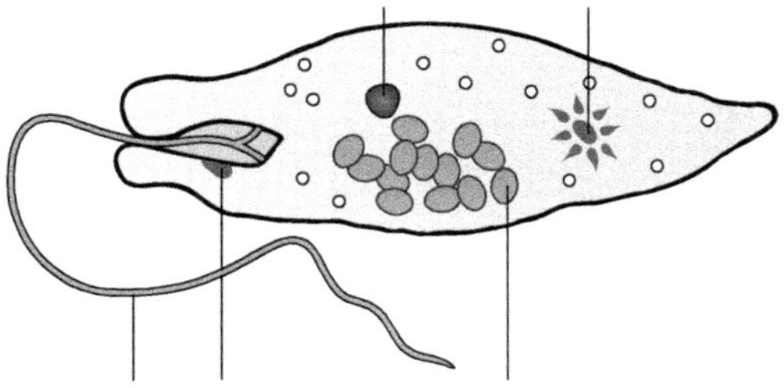

Name the part that:

helps it to move. _____

makes food by photosynthesis. _____

detects light. _____

C Is an **amoeba** more like an animal cell or a plant cell? Circle your answer.

animal cell   **plant cell**

Give **two** reasons to explain your choice.

1 _____

2 _____

What you need to remember

Amoebas and _____ are examples of _____ organisms. This means that they consist of only _____ cell. Both organisms have a cell membrane filled with _____ and contain a nucleus. Euglenas also have _____, which make them look green, an _____ _____ which detects light, and a _____ so they can 'swim'.

Pinchpoint question

Answer the question below, then do the follow-up activity **with the same letter** as the answer you picked.

The main difference between an animal cell and a plant cell is:

A   Only plant cells have cell walls and chloroplasts.

B   All plant cells have chloroplasts.

C   There is no difference.

D   Only animal cells have mitochondria.

Follow-up activities

A   This is a specialised cell from the reproductive system. It is covered in tiny hairs called cilia that move the egg cell along the reproductive tract.

Explain how you can tell that this is an animal cell and **not** a plant cell.

Hint: As well as your reasons for why it is **not** a plant cell, give your reason for why it **is** an animal cell. What is its function? For further help see B1.2 Plant and animal cells.

_____

_____

_____

B   This is a root hair cell. It does **not** contain chloroplasts.

Explain why.

Hint: What is the function of chloroplasts? Where are root hair cells found? For further help see B1.2 Plant and animal cells.

root hair

_____

_____

_____

C Complete the table to show whether the cell components are found in plant or animal cells.

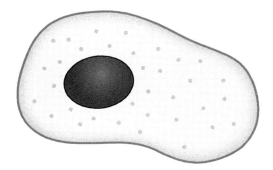 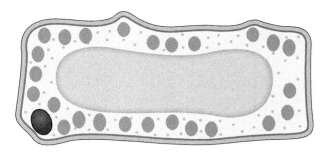

Hint: Some components are found in **both** plant and animal cells. For further help see B1.2 Plant and animal cells.

Cell component	✓ if found in plant cells	✓ if found in animal cells
nucleus		
cell membrane		
cell wall		
cytoplasm		
vacuole		
chloroplast		
mitochondria		

D Complete the following sentences using key words from the box. You may need to use some words more than once or some not at all.

| breathing | energy | organisms | photosynthesis | plant | respiration | sunlight |

Hint: What is the function of mitochondria? For further help see B1 1.2 Plant and animal cells.

Mitochondria are found in both _____ and animal cells. This is where the chemical reaction called _____ takes place.

During this process, _____ is transferred from food for the organism to use for processes such as growth and movement.

Plants can make their own food by _____, whereas animals get their food by eating other organisms. This food is then used during _____.

 Pinchpoint review

Now look back at the question – do you think you chose the right letter?
Turn to the Answers page to find out.

B2.1 Levels of organisation

A The cells of multicellular organisms are organised into levels.

Draw a line to match each level with its description.

tissue	group of different organs working together
organ	group of similar cells working together
organ system	group of different tissues working together

B Using the terms below, complete the diagram to show how the levels of organisation are ordered in a hierarchy.

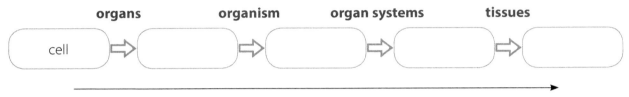

organs   **organism**   **organ systems**   **tissues**

cell ⇨ ⬭ ⇨ ⬭ ⇨ ⬭ ⇨ ⬭

increasing complexity

C Name the organ systems in the diagram below, and give an example of **one** organ found in each system.

Hint: Use the picture to help you.

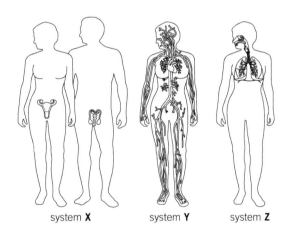

system **X**   system **Y**   system **Z**

system **X** _____   example organ _____

system **Y** _____   example organ _____

system **Z** _____   example organ _____

What you need to remember

_____ organisms have five layers of organisation. This is called a _____. Cells are the building blocks of life. Groups of similar cells working together are called _____ and different tissues working together are called an _____. A group of different organs that work together is called an _____. Finally, an _____ is made up of a number of organ systems working together to perform all the processes needed to stay alive.

B2.2 Gas exchange

A Use the words in the box below to label the diagram of the human respiratory system.

| alveoli | bronchi | bronchiole | diaphragm | lungs | rib | trachea |

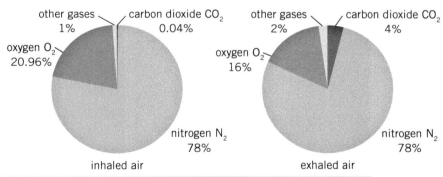

5 _____

1 _____

6 _____

2 _____

7 _____

3 _____

4 _____

B There are millions of alveoli in the lungs. Tick the box(es) below to show how alveoli are able to exchange gases quickly and easily.

Alveoli walls are only one cell thick. ☐   Alveoli create a large surface area. ☐

Alveoli walls are strong and thick. ☐   Alveoli have a poor blood supply. ☐

C These pie charts show the difference in composition of inhaled and exhaled air. Use the data to complete the table below, using the terms **more**, **less**, or **same**.

other gases 1%   carbon dioxide CO_2 0.04%   other gases 2%   carbon dioxide CO_2 4%

oxygen O_2 20.96%   oxygen O_2 16%

nitrogen N_2 78%   nitrogen N_2 78%

inhaled air   exhaled air

Gas	Inhaled air	Exhaled air
carbon dioxide		
nitrogen		
oxygen		

What you need to remember

Breathing is carried out by the _____ system and the major organs of this system are your

_____. When you inhale you take in _____ and when you _____ you

give out carbon dioxide. When you inhale, air travels in through your mouth and nose and then through your

_____. It then travels into your lungs through the _____ and then through a bronchiole,

finally moving into an air sac called an _____. These have thin walls and create a large surface area for

_____ _____, which means that the gases can diffuse in and out of the blood easily.

B2.3 Breathing

A A bell jar model can be used to model what happens during breathing. Add the following labels to the diagram of a bell jar model, to show what each part represents.

| diaphragm | lung | chest cavity | trachea |

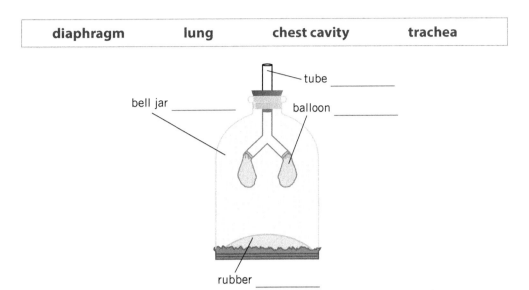

bell jar _____

tube _____

balloon _____

rubber _____

B Circle the correct **bold** words in the sentences below to describe what happens when you **inhale**.

The muscles between your ribs **contract / relax** – this pulls your ribcage **down and in / up and out**.

The diaphragm **contracts / relaxes** – it moves **down / up**.

The volume inside your chest cavity **increases / decreases**.

The pressure inside your chest cavity **increases / decreases**.

This draws air **into / out of** the lungs.

C The statements below can be reordered to explain how you can measure your lung volume. Write down the order of statements you think will give the best method.

Correct order _____

1 Calculate the difference in the water levels – this is your lung volume.

2 Turn the bottle of water upside down in a tank of water.

3 Read the new level of water in the bottle.

4 Read the level of water in the bottle.

5 Take a deep breath, then breathe out for as long as possible into the tube.

6 Fill a plastic bottle full of water and place a plastic tube in the neck of bottle.

What you need to remember

When you inhale, the muscles between your _____ and your diaphragm _____. This _____ the volume of your chest cavity which _____ the pressure, causing air to be drawn in. When you exhale, the muscles _____; this _____ the volume of your chest cavity. This _____ the pressure and forces air _____. You can use a _____ to model this process. Smoking and diseases such as _____ can reduce lung _____.

B2.4 Skeleton

A Together all the bones in your body make up your skeleton.

Label the missing bones using the following words:

| skull | kneecap | vertebral column (backbone) | jaw bone | collar bone | radius | femur |

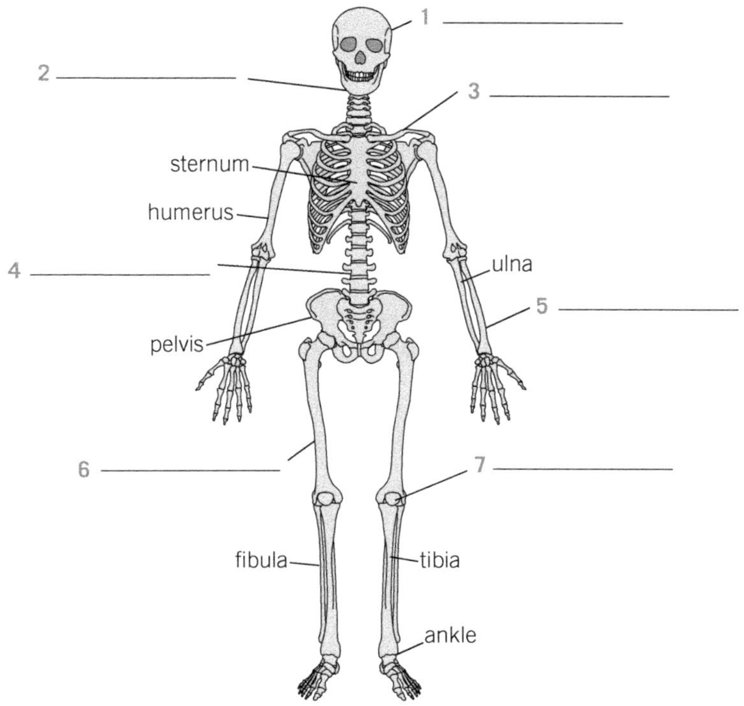

1 _____
2 _____
3 _____
sternum
humerus
4 _____
ulna
5 _____
pelvis
6 _____
7 _____
fibula
tibia
ankle

B Draw a line to match each function of the skeleton with its description.

Function	Description
support	muscles pull on bones to make you move
protection	bones create a framework for muscles and organs to connect to
movement	stop vital organs from being damaged
making blood	tissue in centre of some bones makes blood cells

C Complete the table to show **one** organ that each bone protects.

Bone	Organ protected
skull	
vertebral column	
ribcage	

D Which part of the bone produces blood cells? Tick the correct answer.

spongy bone ☐   bone marrow ☐   compact bone ☐

What you need to remember

Your _____ is made up of bones. The skeleton has four functions: to _____ your organs,

to _____ the body, to help you _____, and to make red and white _____

cells. These cells are made in bone _____, which is found in the centre of some bones.

B2.5 Movement: joints

A Joints are needed for movement.

Tick **one** box to choose the correct description of a joint from the list below.

found where two or more bones join together ☐   smooth layer of tissue ☐

connect muscles to bones ☐   connect muscle to muscle ☐

B Which of the following things occur, to move a bone?

Hint: You may tick more than one box.

muscle relaxes ☐   muscle pulls on bone ☐

muscle contracts ☐   muscle pushes bone ☐

C Draw a line to match the type of joint with how it moves and another line to an example of where this type of joint is found in your body.

Joint	Type of movement	Example
fixed	backwards and forwards	shoulder
ball and socket	no movement	knee
hinge	all directions	skull

D Circle the correct **bold** words in the sentences below to explain how you can carry out simple experiments to measure the force of different body muscles.

The strength of a muscle can be measured by how much **force / strength** it exerts.

You can measure the strength of your muscles using **newton / pascal** scales.

The harder you can push on the scale the **smaller / greater** the force exerted.

Force is measured in newtons. The unit is **N / n**.

What you need to remember

_____ are where bones join together. Different types of joint allow _____ in different

_____. Bones are held together in a joint by _____. The ends of bones in a joint are

covered with _____ to stop them rubbing together. When a muscle _____ it exerts a

_____ on a bone, which is measured in _____ (N), and it pulls the muscle in a certain

direction. This is called biomechanics.

B2.6 Movement: muscles

A Muscles are found all over your body. The major muscle groups used for movement are shown in the diagram.

Select which of the muscle groups is responsible for:

holding your head up _____

bending your arm _____

helping with breathing _____

pointing your toes _____

Hint: Try moving your own muscles.

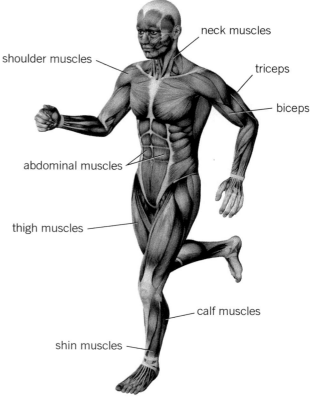

neck muscles

shoulder muscles

triceps

biceps

abdominal muscles

thigh muscles

calf muscles

shin muscles

B Circle the correct **bold** words in the sentences below to give the definition of antagonistic muscles.

A **pair / group** of muscles that work together to control movement at a **bone / joint**.

As one muscle contracts, the other **contracts / relaxes**.

C These diagrams show what happens when the arm bends and straightens.

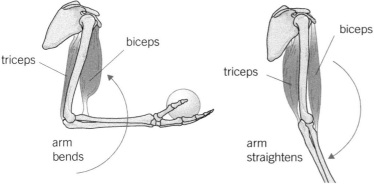

biceps

triceps

arm bends

biceps

triceps

arm straightens

Complete the table with the terms **relaxes** or **contracts** to describe how antagonistic muscles cause the arm movement.

Arm movement	Biceps	Triceps
bends		
straightens		

What you need to remember

Muscles are attached to bones by _____. When a muscle contracts it _____ and

pulls on a _____. Pairs of _____ work together at a _____ to cause

movement. These are called _____ muscles. As one muscle in the pair contracts the other muscle

_____.

B1 Chapter 2 – Pinchpoint

Pinchpoint question

Answer the question below, then do the follow-up activity **with the same letter** as the answer you picked.

Which of the following statements best explains why air enters the lungs when you inhale?

A The diaphragm and ribcage contract and move up. This increases chest volume, drawing air into your lungs.

B The volume of your chest cavity increases. This decreases pressure in your lungs so air is drawn in.

C Your nose and mouth suck air into your lungs when you inhale.

D The volume of your chest cavity increases. This increases air pressure in your lungs so air is drawn in.

Follow-up activities

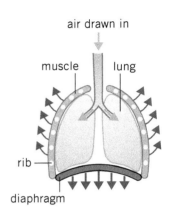

A The diagram shows what happens to the muscles involved in breathing when you inhale.

Complete the table below with a ✓ to show **how** muscle movement increases the volume inside your chest.

Hint: Look at the arrows in the diagram to help you remember the direction the ribs and diaphragm move. For further help see B1 2.3 Breathing.

	Contract	Relax	Move up	Move down
muscles between ribs				
diaphragm				

B The diagram shows a cross section through a bronchiole from a healthy person compared to a person with asthma.

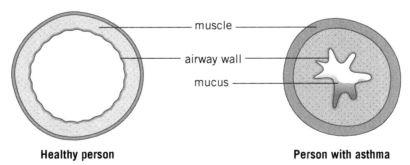

Healthy person   **Person with asthma**

Explain how the differences shown will affect gas exchange in the person with asthma and state what symptom it will cause.

Hint: Which bronchiole will allow the air to flow most easily? For further help see B1 2.2 Gas exchange.

_____

_____

_____

C The bell jar model can be used to help explain what happens when you inhale.

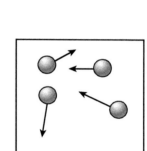

bell jar

tube

balloon

rubber

Complete the following sentences by circling the correct bold words.

Hint: The larger the volume in the bell jar, the lower the pressure inside. For further help see B1 2.3 Breathing.

To 'breathe in' you need to pull the rubber sheet **upwards / downwards**.

This represents your **diaphragm / stomach** contracting.

This **increases / decreases** the volume inside the bell jar.

This makes the pressure inside the bell jar **increase / decrease**.

Air is therefore drawn **in / out**.

D The diagram shows a box full of air molecules. The molecules are all moving in random directions, as shown by the arrows.

a Explain what will happen when one of the molecules strikes the wall of the box. Use the word force in your answer.

Hint: Imagine you are standing in the box and the molecule is a tennis ball. For help see C1 1.7 Gas pressure.

_____

_____

b Now imagine the box is made bigger. Complete the sentences below by circling the correct words.

Hint: The pressure inside the box is linked to how often the molecules strike the walls of their container. For further help see B1 2.3 Breathing and C1 1.7 Gas pressure.

When the box is bigger, the molecules will strike the walls **more / less** often.

This **increases / decreases** the pressure inside the box.

This is what happens when you breathe **in / out**.

 Pinchpoint review

Now look back at the question – do you think you chose the right letter?
Turn to the Answers page to find out.

B3.1 Adolescence

A The time during which you change from a child to an adult is known as adolescence.

Circle the correct **bold** words in the sentences below.

Adolescence / Puberty involves both emotional and physical changes.

These changes are caused by **nerve impulses / sex hormones**.

The physical changes which take place are called **adolescence / puberty**.

Puberty takes place between the ages of **9–14 / 15–18** in most people.

B Girls and boys undergo a number of physical changes during puberty.

Put a **tick** (✓) against the statements below to show whether they occur in boys or girls.

Physical change	Boys	Girls
breasts develop		
voice deepens		
periods start		
hips widen		
shoulders widen		
testes start to produce sperm		
ovaries start to release egg cells		

C A number of physical changes occur in **both** males and females during puberty.

Describe two of these changes.

Change 1 _____

Change 2 _____

What you need to remember

The period of time when a person develops from a child into an adult is known as _____.

The _____ changes that take place are called _____. These changes are caused by

_____. Both males and females grow _____ and get

_____ hair. Boys' voices _____ and their _____ widen. Girls will start

their _____ and their _____ widen.

B3.2 Reproductive systems

A Label the main structures of the female reproductive system. Use the words in the box below.

cervix	ovary	oviduct	uterus	vagina

3 _____
4 _____
2 _____
1 _____
5 _____

B Label the main structures of the male reproductive system. Use the words in the box below.

glands	penis	scrotum	sperm duct	testis	urethra

3 _____
2 _____
1 _____
4 _____
5 _____
6 _____

C Draw a line to match each part of the female reproductive system with its function.

ovaries	where a baby develops until it is born
uterus	receives sperm during sexual intercourse
oviducts	carry egg to uterus
vagina	contain eggs

D Draw a line to match each part of the male reproductive system with its function.

penis	produce nutrients to keep sperm alive
glands	places sperm in vagina
sperm ducts	produce sperm
testes	carry sperm from testes to penis

What you need to remember

The function of the male reproductive system is to make _____ cells and release them inside a

female's _____. Sperm are made in the _____, which are contained in the scrotum.

They then pass through the _____ and urethra, and are then released from the

_____ during sexual intercourse. The function of the female reproductive system is

to release _____ cells from the ovaries. An egg passes through the _____ to the

_____. If a pregnancy occurs, this is where a baby grows and develops.

B3.3 Fertilisation and implantation

A Gametes are reproductive cells.

Circle the correct **bold** words in the sentences below about female gametes.

The female gamete is called an **egg / baby** cell.

Every **day / month** an egg cell is released from **the uterus / an ovary** into one of the oviducts.

These tubes are lined with tiny hairs called **cilia / root hairs**. These waft the egg along the tube towards the **ovary / uterus** as the egg cell cannot move on its own.

B Circle **true** or **false** for the following statements about sperm cells.

1	The male gamete is called a sperm cell.	**true / false**
2	Sperm cells are made in the ovaries.	**true / false**
3	Sperm cells have a tail to swim.	**true / false**
4	Sperm cells are released from the penis.	**true / false**
5	Sperm cells are released into the uterus.	**true / false**

C Draw a line to match each term to its definition.

fertilisation	semen containing sperm is released into the vagina
ejaculation	the embryo attaches to the lining of the uterus
implantation	the nuclei of the sperm and egg cell join together

D Where is fertilisation most likely to occur?

Tick the correct answer.

ovary ☐   vagina ☐

uterus ☐   oviduct ☐

What you need to remember

_____ are reproductive cells. The male gamete is called a _____ cell and the female gamete is called an _____ cell. Every month an egg is released from an _____ and wafted along the oviduct by tiny hairs called _____. During sexual intercourse, sperm are released into the vagina. This is known as _____. The sperm swim towards the egg in the oviduct. To create a new organism the _____ of the sperm and egg cell need to join together. This is called _____. The fertilised egg then divides to form a ball of cells called an _____. The embryo attaches to the lining of the _____ and begins to develop into a baby. This is called _____.

B3.4 Development of a fetus

A Circle the correct **bold** words in the sentences below to describe pregnancy.

The period of time an organism develops in the uterus between fertilisation and birth is known as **gestation / development**.

In humans this lasts for around **9 / 12** months and is also known as pregnancy.

To grow, a fetus needs nutrients and oxygen. It receives these from its mother, through her **stomach / blood**.

B After eight weeks of growth, the embryo is called a fetus. Label the main structures in the diagram opposite using the words in the box below.

cervix	fetus	fluid sac	placenta
	umbilical cord	uterus	

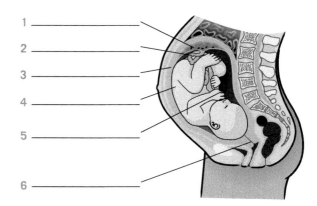

1 _____

2 _____

3 _____

4 _____

5 _____

6 _____

C Draw a line to match each of the following structures with its function.

placenta	connects the fetus to the placenta
umbilical cord	acts as a shock absorber protecting the fetus from any bumps
fluid sac	keeps the fetus in the uterus until it is ready to be born
cervix	organ where substances pass between mother's and fetus's blood

D Circle the correct **bold** words in the sentences below to describe what happens during birth.

When a baby is ready to be born, the mother's cervix **contracts / relaxes**.
The muscles in the wall of the **vagina / uterus** contract.

The baby is pushed out of its mother's body through the **vagina / oviduct**.

What you need to remember

The period of time an organism develops in the _____ is known as _____. In humans

this is about _____ months. The fetus develops inside a fluid _____. This protects the

fetus from any bumps. During this time the fetus receives nutrients and _____ from the mother.

These pass from the mother's blood to the fetus's _____ in the _____. The fetus is

connected to the placenta by the _____. During birth the mother's

_____ relaxes and the _____ wall contracts, pushing the baby out of the body through

the _____.

B3.5 The menstrual cycle

A Reorder the statements below, to describe the main stages in the menstrual cycle.

Hint: Start at day 1, when the period occurs.

Correct order ☐ ☐ ☐ ☐

1 Ovulation occurs.

2 If the egg is unfertilised the lining starts to break down.

3 Bleeding stops and the lining of the uterus starts to thicken.

4 Blood from the lining of the uterus leaves the body.

B Choose from the words in the box to complete the sentences below.

fertilised	menstrual	ovulation	period	uterus

Females have a monthly cycle during which the _____ lining thickens and then breaks down, leaving the body if an egg is not _____. This is called the _____ cycle.

The cycle starts with a _____. This is when the old uterus lining is lost through the vagina. The uterus lining then regrows.

An egg cell is released in the middle of the cycle; this is called _____.

C Around which day of the menstrual cycle is ovulation most likely to occur?

day 1 ☐   **day 5** ☐

day 14 ☐   **day 28** ☐

D If the egg **is** fertilised, what changes will occur in a woman's body? You may tick more than one option.

uterus lining will remain thick ☐   periods will occur ☐

uterus lining will break down ☐   periods will stop ☐

E Name **two** methods that can be used to prevent pregnancy.

Method 1 _____   **Method 2** _____

What you need to remember

The female reproductive system works in a cycle called the _____ cycle. Each month an _____ is released. This is called _____. If this is not fertilised the uterus _____ breaks down and leaves the body. This is called a _____. The cycle then begins again.

B3.6 Flowers and pollination

A Complete the labels of the flower structures using the words in the box below.

anther	filament	ovary	petal
	sepal	stigma	style

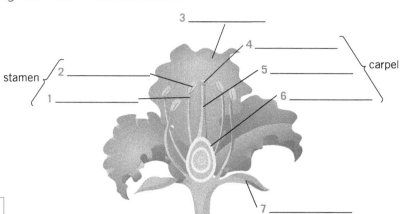

3 _____

4 _____

stamen 2 _____

1 _____

5 _____ } carpel

6 _____

7 _____

B Draw a line to match each flower structure with its function.

anther		sticky to 'catch' pollen

stigma		produces pollen

ovary		contains ovules

C Which is the correct definition of **pollination?** Tick (✓) your answer.

When the pollen and ovule join together. ☐

Transfer of pollen from the anther to the stigma. ☐

Fusion of nuclei of pollen and ovule. ☐

D Complete the table to show the main features of a wind-pollinated and an insect-pollinated plant. Tick (✓) the column you would find each feature in.

Feature	✓ Wind-pollinated	✓ Insect-pollinated
brightly coloured flowers		
large quantities of pollen		
pollen with low mass		
nectar		
brown or dull green flowers		
sweet-smelling flowers		
anther and stigma inside the flower		
anther and stigma hang outside the flower		

What you need to remember

Pollination is the name given to the transfer of _____ from the _____ to the stigma.

Pollen can be carried by the wind or by _____. To attract insects, flowers are often _____

coloured, contain _____ and are _____ smelling. Wind-pollinated plants produce

_____ amounts of _____ pollen. Their anthers and _____ hang outside

the flower.

A **a** Label the diagram of the first stage of fertilisation using the words in the box below.

   b Then draw on the diagram and add a label to describe what happens next to allow fertilisation to occur.

ovule	ovule nucleus	pollen grain	pollen nucleus

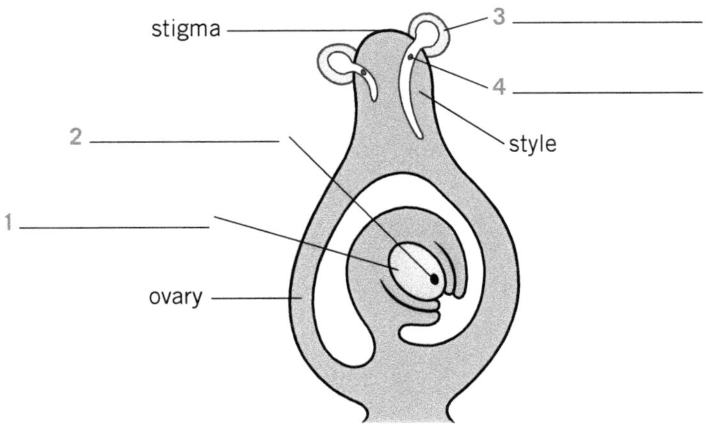

stigma

3 _____

4 _____

style

2 _____

1 _____

ovary

B Circle the correct **bold** words in the sentences below to the process of fertilisation.

If the pollen grain lands on the **stigma / anther** of the correct species it grows a **tail / pollen tube**.

This grows down the **stigma / style** until it reaches an **ovule / seed** inside the ovary.

The nucleus of the pollen grain then travels down the tube and joins with the ovule nucleus. This is called **germination / fertilisation**.

The ovary then develops into the **seeds / fruit** and the ovules become **seeds / fruit**.

C Which of the following things do seeds need to germinate? You may tick more than one box.

water ☐   oxygen ☐   light ☐

carbon dioxide ☐   warmth ☐   soil ☐

What you need to remember

During _____, the nucleus of the _____ grain and the _____ join together. The ovary then develops into the _____ and the ovules become _____.

To create a new plant, the seed needs to _____. For this to occur it needs _____, water, and oxygen.

B3.8 Seed dispersal

A Tick the correct definition of seed dispersal.

The joining together of pollen and ovule nuclei to make a seed. ☐

The period of time when a seed starts to grow. ☐

The movement of seeds away from the parent plant. ☐

B Draw a line to match each method of seed dispersal with an adaptation of seeds dispersed in this way.

wind	fruits burst open when they are ripe, throwing seeds in different directions
animal (internally)	small mass allowing them to float
animal (externally)	small mass and extensions that act as parachutes or wings
water	seeds contained in bright, sweet fruits
explosive	hooks to attach to fur

C Name the method of seed dispersal used by the following seeds.

a

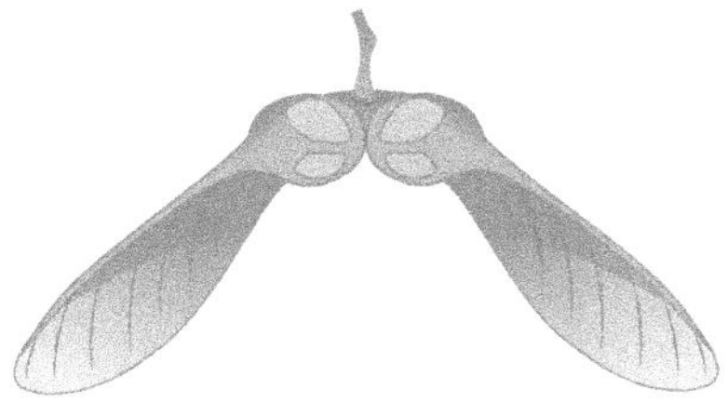

b

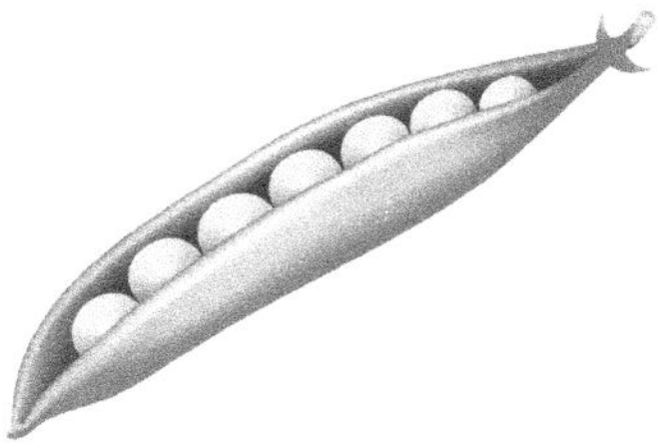

method _____   method _____

D A group of students carried out an investigation into seed dispersal by the wind. They tested the hypothesis, 'the larger the wing of the seed, the further it will travel'.

Identify the variables used in this investigation.

independent variable _____

dependent variable _____

control variable _____

What you need to remember

Seeds are _____ away from the parent plant to reduce _____. This increases their

chances of survival as they have more _____ and nutrients to grow. Seeds can be dispersed by the

_____, explosion, _____, and water.

31

Pinchpoint question

Answer the question below, then do the follow-up activity **with the same letter** as the answer you picked.

Which of the following statements best explains the role of the placenta during pregnancy?

A   To transfer substances between the mother's and the fetus's blood.

B   To transfer oxygen so the fetus can breathe.

C   To transfer blood, which contains useful substances, between the mother and the fetus.

D   To prevent any substances from reaching the fetus.

Follow-up activities

A   Like other gas exchange surfaces, the placenta is adapted for gas exchange.

Use the diagram and your knowledge to suggest how the placenta is adapted to maximise diffusion.

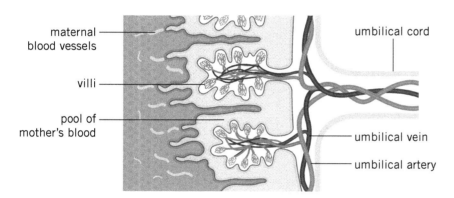

Hint: For further help see B1 3.4 Development of a fetus and B1 1.4 Movement of substances.

_____

_____

_____

_____

B   Complete the following sentences using the appropriate **bold** words.

You breathe to take **oxygen / carbon dioxide** into your lungs for respiration and exhale the waste product **oxygen / carbon dioxide**.

A baby does not take its first breath until after it is **conceived / born**.

In the uterus the fetus's lungs are filled with **air / fluid**.

In order to **respire / photosynthesise** to transfer energy for growth, the fetus needs to receive **water / glucose** and **oxygen / carbon dioxide** from its mother.

These substances are carried in the mother's blood to the **cervix / placenta**.

Inside this organ they **diffuse / flow** into the fetus's blood.

Hint: For further help see B1 3.4 Development of a fetus.

C Read the statements below. Look at the diagram and use your own knowledge to circle **true** or **false** for each statement.

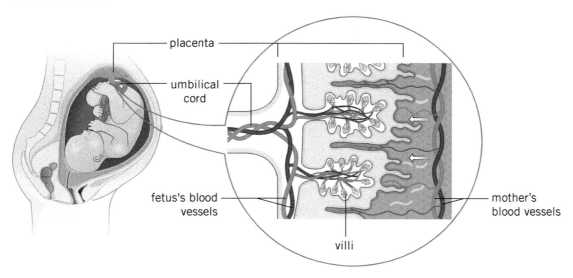

1 The fetus is surrounded by air to protect it from bumps.   **true / false**

2 The umbilical cord attaches the fetus to the placenta.   **true / false**

3 The fetus grows inside one of the mother's ovaries.   **true / false**

4 The umbilical cord contains the mother's blood vessels.   **true / false**

5 The maternal and fetal blood mix.   **true / false**

6 Substances pass between the fetal and maternal blood in the placenta.   **true / false**

Hint: For further help see B1 3.4 Development of a fetus.

D Complete the table by placing a **tick** (✓) in the correct column, to show which substances pass into the fetus's blood from the mother's blood, and which pass into the mother's blood from the fetus's blood.

Substance	Mother → fetus	Fetus → mother
oxygen		
carbon dioxide		
urea (waste)		
glucose		
antibodies (prevent disease)		

Hint: For further help see B1 3.4 Development of a fetus.

  Pinchpoint review

Now look back at the question – do you think you chose the right letter?
Turn to the Answers page to find out.

B1 Revision questions

1 **a** 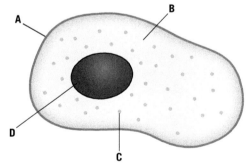 Identify the following structures as part of either the male or female reproductive system by writing them in the correct column of the table. **(2 marks)**

ovary   oviduct   penis   sperm duct   testis   uterus

Female reproductive system	Male reproductive system

b During puberty, the male and female reproductive systems develop to be able to produce a baby.

  i Name **one** change that **only** occurs in girls.
  (1 mark)

  _____

  ii Name **one** change that **only** occurs in boys.
  (1 mark)

  _____

  iii Name **one** change that occurs in **both** boys and girls. **(1 mark)**

  _____

2 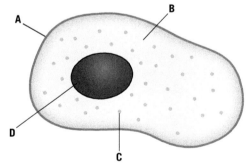 **Figure 1** shows an animal cell.

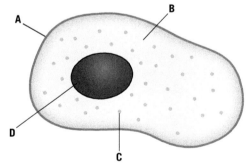

Figure 1

a Name the structures **A**, **B**, **C**, and **D**. **(4 marks)**

  A _____

  B _____

  C _____

  D _____

b Name **two** structures that you would find in a plant cell, but **not** in an animal cell. **(2 marks)**

  1 _____

  2 _____

c Name the piece of equipment you could use to view a cell. **(1 mark)**

  _____

3 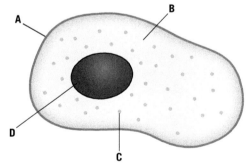 Organisms are made up of a number of smaller structures.

a List the structures in order of size, from smallest to largest, to show the organisation of structures of an organism. **(4 marks)**

  organ   tissue   cell   organism   organ system

  _____

  _____

b Look at the following list of organs and answer the following questions.

  bone   brain   leaf   lung   pancreas   stomach

  i Name an organ in the digestive system.
  (1 mark)

  _____

  ii Name an organ in the human gas exchange system. **(1 mark)**

  _____

  iii Name a plant organ. **(1 mark)**

  _____

4 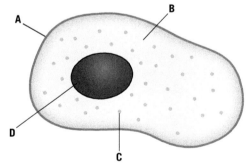 Specialised cells have a special shape and structure to carry out a specific function.

a Draw a line to match each cell to its special feature. **(2 marks)**

sperm cell	lots of chloroplasts
leaf cell	fat store
egg cell	tail

b Name one other example of:

  i a specialised animal cell _____ **(1 mark)**

  ii a specialised plant cell _____ **(1 mark)**

5 🧪🧪 **Figure 2** shows a flower.

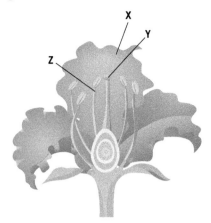

Figure 2

a Name the structures **X**, **Y**, and **Z**. (**3 marks**)

X _____

Y _____

Z _____

b Pollen and ovules are the plant gametes.

i Define the word **gamete**. (**1 mark**)

_____

ii Name the part of the flower where pollen is made. (**1 mark**)

_____

iii Name the part of the flower where ovules are found. (**1 mark**)

_____

c Give **two** different ways in which a plant can be pollinated and give an example of a plant which is pollinated by each method. (**2 marks**)

1 _____ **example:** _____

2 _____ **example:** _____

d To produce a seed, fertilisation must occur.

Describe what happens during the process of fertilisation. (**2 marks**)

_____

_____

_____

6 🧪🧪 Plant and animal cells contain smaller structures.

a Draw a line from each plant cell structure to its correct function. (**3 marks**)

nucleus		stores sap and helps to keep the cell firm
vacuole		controls the activities of the cell
cytoplasm		where the cell's chemical reactions take place

b Explain why plant cells contain chloroplasts.

(**1 mark**)

_____

_____

7 🧪🧪 A group of students wanted to observe some onion cells under a microscope.

a Explain how the students should set up and use the microscope so they can view the cells clearly. (**6 marks**)

_____

_____

_____

_____

_____

_____

_____

_____

_____

_____

b Sketch a diagram below, showing what you would expect the students to see through the microscope. Label **three** cell components. (**4 marks**)

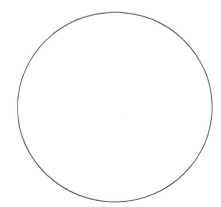

c Plant cells have a cell wall.

   i Write down what cell walls are made from.

       (1 mark)

   _____

   ii Explain the function of the cell wall. **(2 marks)**

   _____

   _____

8 🧪🧪 **Figure 3** shows a structure found in your lungs

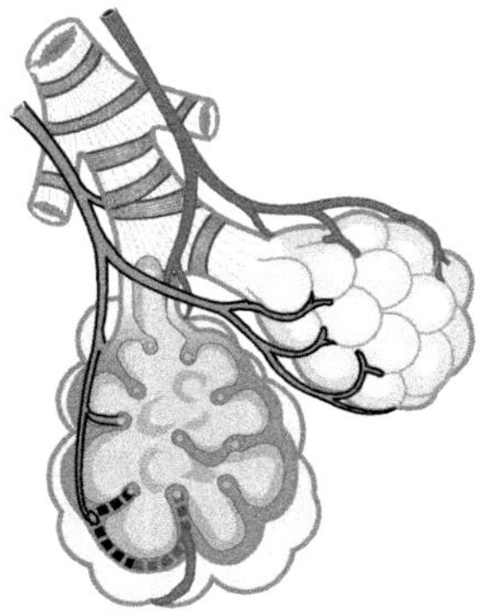

Figure 3

a Name the structure that forms the gas exchange surface. **(1 mark)**

   _____

b Describe this structure's role in gas exchange.

       (2 marks)

   _____

   _____

c Explain how this structure is adapted to perform its function. **(3 marks)**

   _____

   _____

   _____

   _____

9 🧪🧪 A student measured his lung volume using the equipment shown in **Figure 4**.

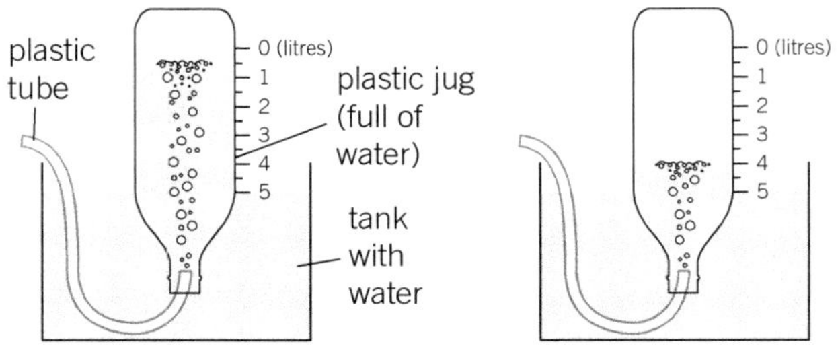

Figure 4

a Calculate the volume of air exhaled by the student. **(2 marks)**

   _____ litres

b Write down **two** differences between the air exhaled by the student, and the air inhaled. **(2 marks)**

   1 _____

   2 _____

c Suggest **one** factor that could reduce the student's lung volume. **(1 mark)**

   _____

10 🧪🧪 Hermione measured the force of her triceps muscle by pushing down onto a set of bathroom scales, measuring the force in newtons. **Table 1** shows her results.

Table 1

Force measurement 1 (N)	Force measurement 2 (N)	Force measurement 3 (N)
450	410	370

a Calculate the mean force from Hermione's triceps muscle. Remember to state the units. **(3 marks)**

   _____

b Suggest **one** reason why each force measurement was different. **(1 mark)**

   _____

   _____

c The biceps and triceps muscles are found in the upper arm, as shown in **Figure 5**.

biceps
triceps
arm
bends

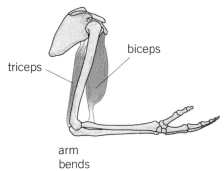

Figure 5

Explain how these muscles work together to move your lower arm upwards and downwards. **(3 marks)**

11 Basil is an edible plant. A group of students were asked to investigate the conditions needed for basil seeds to germinate. They placed seeds onto cotton wool, in the conditions shown in **Figure 6**.

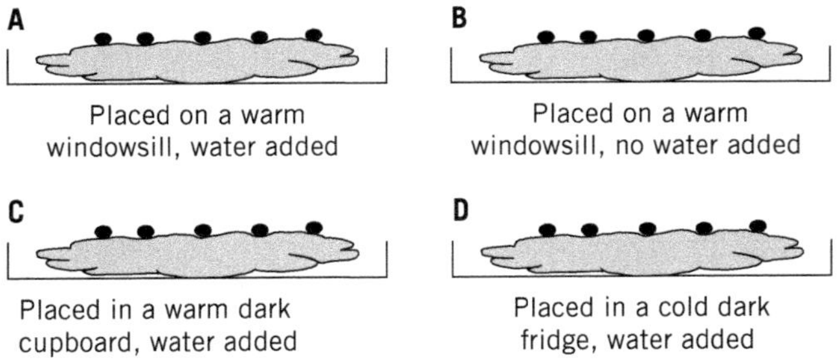

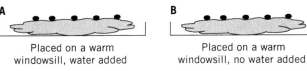

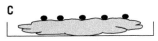

A
Placed on a warm windowsill, water added
B
Placed on a warm windowsill, no water added
C
Placed in a warm dark cupboard, water added
D
Placed in a cold dark fridge, water added

Figure 6

a Circle each dish where you would expect germination to occur. **(2 marks)**

b The students used a total of 20 seeds. Only 8 of these germinated.

Calculate the percentage of seeds that germinated. **(2 marks)**

__________%

c Basil seeds have a sticky outer layer, called mucilage. Suggest and explain how basil seeds are dispersed. **(2 marks)**

12 During pregnancy, a baby develops inside its mother's uterus.

a Name the structure which keeps the baby in the uterus until it is ready to be born. **(1 mark)**

b Describe the function of the fluid sac. **(1 mark)**

c Describe the role of the placenta. **(4 marks)**

B1 Checklist

Revision question number	Outcome	Topic reference	☹	😐	☺
1a	Name the parts of the male and female human reproductive systems.	B1 3.2			
1b	State changes to the bodies of boys and girls during puberty.	B1 3.1			
2a	Identify and name parts of an animal cell.	B1 1.2			
2b	Give the differences between a plant and an animal cell.	B1 1.2			
2c	Name the equipment required to observe very small structures, including cells.	B1 1.1			
3a	Order structures in a multicellular organism from smallest to largest.	B1 2.1			
3b	List the organs found in a given organ system.	B1 2.1			
4a	State specialised features of plant and animal cells.	B1 1.3			
4b	Name some examples of specialised plant and animal cells.	B1 1.3			
5a	Identify the main structures in a flower.	B1 3.6			
5b	State the definition of 'gamete'. State the function of parts of a flower.	B1 3.3 B1 3.6			
5c	Name two different ways in which a plant can be pollinated.	B1 3.6			
5d	Describe the process of fertilisation.	B1 3.7			
6a	Match some components of a cell to their functions.	B1 1.2			
6b	State the function of chloroplasts.	B1 1.2			
7a	Explain how to use a microscope to observe a cell.	B1 1.1			
7b	Sketch a plant cell as it would appear through a microscope and label the structures.	B1 1.2			
7c	Describe the structure and function of cell components.	B1 1.2			
8a	Identify structures in the gas exchange system.	B1 2.2			
8b	Describe the role of the alveoli in gas exchange.	B1 2.2			
8c	Describe how parts of the gas exchange system are adapted to their function.	B1 2.2			
9a	Calculate lung volume from the results of an experiment.	B1 2.3 🧮			
9b	Describe the differences between inhaled and exhaled air.	B1 2.2			
9c	Suggest factors that could affect lung volume.	B1 2.3			
10a	Calculate a mean from repeat measurements.	WS 1.3 🧮 B1 2.5			
10b	Suggest reasons for variation in experimental data.	WS 1.5 / B1 2.5			
10c	Explain how muscles work together to produce movement.	B1 2.6			
11a	Describe the conditions required for seed germination.	B1 3.7			
11b	Use data to calculate percentage germination.	B1 3.7 🧮			
11c	Describe methods of seed dispersal.	B1 3.8			
12a, b, c	Describe the role of female reproductive structures during pregnancy.	B1 3.4			

C1.1 The particle model

A Draw a line to match each key word with its meaning.

materials	made of just one type of material, every particle is the same
substances	what a material looks like and how it behaves
properties	the tiny things that everything is made from
particles	the different types of stuff that everything is made from

B The table gives some information about particles in two substances, gold and silver.

Substance	Radius of particle (nm)	Relative mass of particle
gold	0.144	197
silver	0.144	108

The diagrams show how the particles are arranged in gold and silver.

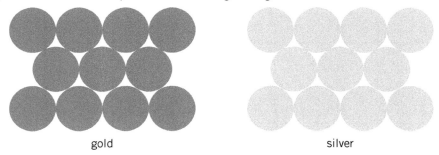

gold   silver

Circle the correct **bold** words in the sentences below.

The table shows that a gold particle is **bigger than / the same size as** a silver particle.

The diagrams show that the particles are arranged **the same / differently** in gold and silver.

The table shows that a gold particle has a **greater / smaller** mass than a silver particle. This means that a 1 cm³ cube of gold has a **greater / smaller** mass than a 1 cm³ cube of silver.

C Harry has a sample of ice and a sample of liquid water.

Complete the table to show which sample is which.

Sample	How the particles are arranged	Is the sample ice or liquid water?
Y	The particles can slide over each other.	
Z	The particles do not move around.	

What you need to remember

Materials are made up of tiny _____. Many materials are mixtures of different substances. Different

substances are made from _____ particles. The properties of a substance describe what it

_____ like and how it _____. Every substance has its own properties. The properties

of a substance depend on what its particles are like, how its particles are _____, and how its particles

_____ around.

C1.2 States of matter

A A substance has different properties in each of its three states.

Tick the statements that are true.

1 A solid does not flow. ☐
2 You can compress a liquid. ☐
3 A liquid flows. ☐
4 A gas takes the shape of the bottom of its container. ☐
5 A gas does not flow. ☐

B Draw a line to match each particle diagram to the state that it shows.

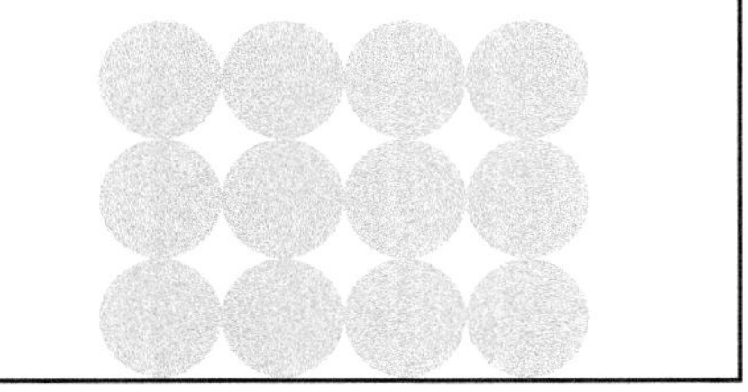

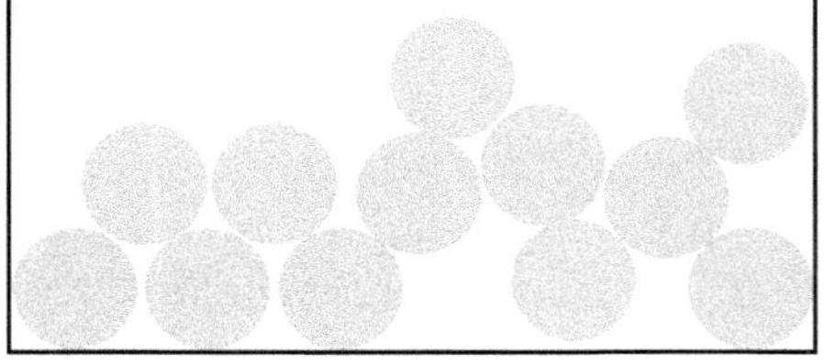

| solid | liquid | gas |

C Write down **three** correct sentences from the sentence starters and endings below.

A solid does not flow	because its particles touch each other.
A gas has no fixed shape	because its particles do not move around.
You cannot easily compress a liquid	because its particles move around.

_____

_____

_____

_____

_____

_____

What you need to remember

Most substances can exist in the solid state, the liquid state, and the _____ state. These are the three

states of _____. The particles of a substance in each of its three states are the same. In each of the

three states of matter, the arrangement and _____ of the particles are _____.

C1.3 Melting and freezing

A Draw a line to match each change of state to its definition.

Use only **two** of the definitions.

Change of state

melting

freezing

Definition

the change of state from liquid to solid

the change of state from gas to liquid

the change of state from solid to liquid

B A substance is in the solid state at room temperature (20 °C) if its melting point is higher than 20 °C.
Write down the names of **two** substances from the table that are solid at room temperature.

Substance	Melting point (°C)
bromine	−7
neon	−249
sodium	98
titanium	1670

1 _____ 2 _____

C A student heats a substance that starts off in the solid state.

The student plots the graph opposite.

Label the graph by writing the numbers of **two** labels in each box.

1 The solid is getting warmer.

2 The liquid is getting warmer.

3 The solid is melting.

4 The particles are moving out of and away from their places in the pattern.

5 The particles are vibrating more and more quickly.

6 The particles are moving around more and more quickly.

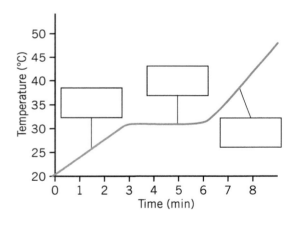

What you need to remember

The change of state from solid to liquid is called _____ . When a solid warms up, its particles vibrate

_____ . The solid melts when its particles move _____ from their places in the

pattern. A substance melts at its _____ point. A _____ substance has a sharp

melting point. The change of state from a liquid to a solid is called _____ . When a liquid cools, its

particles move around more _____ . It freezes when its particles get into a regular pattern and

vibrate in fixed positions.

C1.4 Boiling

A The statements below describe how to do an experiment to find the boiling point of water but they are in the wrong order.

Read the statements and write down the order of instructions you think describes the experiment best.

Correct order ☐ ☐ ☐ ☐ ☐

1 Pour some water into a beaker.

2 When the water is bubbling fast and there are bubbles everywhere in the water use a thermometer to measure the temperature.

3 Place the beaker of water on a tripod and gauze with a Bunsen burner underneath.

4 Use the lighted Bunsen burner to heat the water.

5 Light the Bunsen burner.

B Draw a line to match each sentence starter with the correct ending.

When water boils	touch other particles.
Boiling water has water in	are spread out.
In boiling water, the particles in the liquid	bubbles of steam form everywhere in the liquid.
In boiling water, the particles in the bubbles of steam	escape to the air.
In boiling water, steam bubbles rise to the surface of liquid and	both the liquid and gas states.

C A substance is in the gas state at room temperature (20 °C) if its melting point and boiling point are lower than 20 °C.

Complete the table to show the state of each substance at room temperature.

Substance	Melting point (°C)	Boiling point (°C)	State at room temperature (solid, liquid, or gas)
hexane	−94	68	
xenon	−112	−108	
yttrium	1500	2930	
zirconium	1850	3580	

What you need to remember

A substance can change from the liquid to the _____ state by boiling. Boiling happens when

bubbles of the substance in the _____ state form everywhere in the liquid and rise to the surface to

escape into the air. The total mass of the gas and _____ is the same as the mass of the liquid at the

start. Scientists say the mass is _____ in boiling. A substance boils at a certain temperature and this is

called its _____ point.

C1.5 More changes of state

A Draw a line to match each change of state to its name.

Change of state

| liquid to gas |

| solid to gas |

| gas to liquid |

Name

| sublimation |

| condensation |

| evaporation or boiling |

B Circle the correct **bold** words in the sentences below.

In evaporation, particles leave from the liquid **surface / bottom** only. In boiling, bubbles of gas form **everywhere in / on the surface of** the liquid.

When a gas cools, its particles move more and more **quickly / slowly** and get **closer together / further apart**. When the particles are touching each other, a liquid forms.

The change from gas to liquid is called **evaporation / condensation**.

C A student investigates how quickly drops of water evaporate in different places.

He sets up the apparatus below.

drop of water   Petri dish

The student puts each Petri dish in a different place: one on top of a heater, one in a fridge, and one on a windowsill. He measures the time taken for all the water to evaporate from each dish.

Draw a line to match each variable to its variable type in this investigation.

| place (where the Petri dish is) |

| amount of water |

| time for all the water to evaporate |

| control variable |

| independent variable |

| dependent variable |

What you need to remember

A substance can change from the liquid to the _____ state by evaporation or boiling. Evaporation

happens when particles leave the _____ of a liquid. The change of state from gas to liquid is called

_____. The change of state from solid to gas is called _____.

43

C1.6 Diffusion

A Tick the descriptions below that are examples of diffusion.

Description	✓ if it is an example of diffusion
the smell of perfume reaching your nose from someone's neck	
sugar mixing with tea when you stir it	
a drop of ink spreading through water without stirring	

B A student investigates the diffusion of purple potassium manganate(VII) when it dissolves in water. She wants to find out how water temperature affects the time for the purple colour to spread out. She sets up the apparatus below.

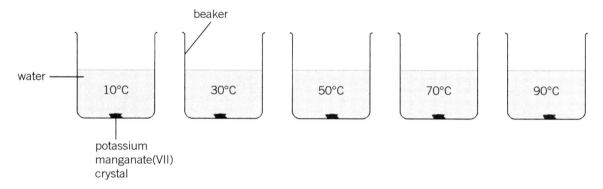

Circle the correct **bold** words in the sentences below.

The student changes the temperature, so temperature is the **independent / dependent** variable.

The student measures the time for the purple colour to spread through the water. This means that time is the **independent / dependent** variable in this investigation.

The student keeps the volume of water the same. This means that the volume of water is a **dependent / control** variable.

C Edward puts some flowers in the corner of a room.

Half an hour later, he can smell the flowers wherever he is in the room.

Add some particles to the diagram to show why he can smell the flowers everywhere in the room.

Draw each particle as a small circle.

What you need to remember

The random movement and _____ of particles is called diffusion. Diffusion happens in the liquid

and _____ states because the particles in these states move around all the time. An example of

_____ is when a drop of ink spreads through water. The particles move by themselves. You do not

need to shake or _____ .

C1.7 Gas pressure

A Circle the correct **bold** words in the sentences below.

When a substance is in the gas state, its particles move around the **bottom of the / whole** container.

The particles move randomly **up and down / in all directions**. The particles hit each other and **all the / the top and bottom** walls of the container.

The collisions with **other particles / the walls** exert a force on the walls. The force per unit **area / volume** on the wall surface is called the gas pressure.

B The diagrams show some identical particles in two jars.

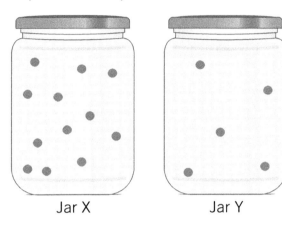

Jar X   Jar Y

Tick the statements that are true.

1 If you increase the temperature of jar Y, the pressure inside it increases. ☐

2 The pressure in jar X is less than the pressure in jar Y, if they are both at the same temperature. ☐

3 If you decrease the temperature of jar X, the pressure inside it increases. ☐

4 The pressure in jar Y is less than the pressure in jar X, if they are both at the same temperature. ☐

C Draw a line to match each sentence starter with the correct ending. You might need to use some endings twice, and some not at all.

The greater the number of gas particles in a container,	the pressure decreases.
If you remove some gas particles from a container,	the higher the pressure.
The higher the temperature of a gas in a container,	the pressure increases.
If you heat up a gas in its container,	the lower the pressure.

What you need to remember

The particles in a gas move randomly in _____ directions. When they move, they may hit – or

_____ with – the walls of the container. The collisions exert a _____ on the walls. The

force per unit area acting on a surface is the gas _____.

Pinchpoint question

Answer the question below, then do the follow-up activity **with the same letter** as the answer you picked.

Jack puts some water in a blocked syringe. He pushes hard on the plunger. Which statement best describes and explains his observations?

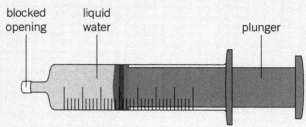

A   The volume of water decreases because the particles get smaller.

B   The volume of water stays the same because its particles cannot get closer together.

C   The volume of water decreases because the particles get closer together.

D   The volume of water stays the same because the particles move around all the time, sliding over each other.

Follow-up activities

A   Circle the correct **bold** words in the sentences below.

Water can exist in **three / two** states: as a solid, as a liquid, and as a gas. In each state, the particles of water are **the same size / different sizes**. The particles in the three states are **different / identical** in every way, and their size and shape **never / often** change, even when you apply a force. But some of the properties of ice, liquid water, and steam are **the same / different**. There are two reasons for this:

- the particles are arranged **differently / in the same** way in each state

- the particles move **differently / in the same way** in each state.

Hint: What changes when solid ice becomes liquid water? Do the particles themselves change? For help see C1 1.2 States of matter.

B   Jack has some air in a blocked syringe. Air is a gas.

Complete the diagram on the right to show what happens when Jack presses on the plunger.

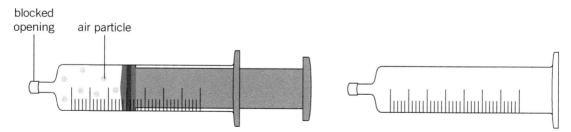

Hint: You need to draw the position of the plunger and some particles. How does the distance between the particles change? For help see C1 1.2 States of matter.

C Keira draws some particles in liquid water.

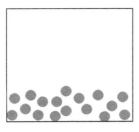

a i Write down **two** things that she has drawn correctly in her drawing.

1 _____

2 _____

ii Write down **one** thing that she has drawn incorrectly. _____

b In the box, draw the correct arrangement of particles in liquid water.

Hint: How close together are the particles in a liquid? For help see C1 1.2 States of matter.

D Draw a line to match each observation to the **one best** explanation.

Observation	Explanation
a liquid flows	its particles can get closer together
a liquid cannot be compressed (squashed)	its particles move around, sliding over each other
a gas can be compressed	its particles are in fixed positions
a gas has no fixed shape	its particles cannot get closer together
a solid does not change shape unless it melts or breaks	its particles move around in the whole container

Hint: There are two explanations that describe the particles in liquid and two that describe the particles in gas, but only one of these statements actually explains each observation. Think carefully about which explanation best explains each observation. For help see C1 1.2 States of matter.

 Pinchpoint review

Now look back at the question – do you think you chose the right letter?
Turn to the Answers page to find out.

C2.1 Elements

A Tick the statements below that are true.

1 There are millions of elements. ☐
2 An element cannot be broken down into other substances. ☐
3 Oxygen is an element. ☐
4 The chemical symbol for magnesium is MG. ☐
5 Scientists in the UK and Russia use different chemical symbols for the element iron. ☐

B Draw a line to match each element name to its chemical symbol.

hydrogen	He
carbon	Fe
helium	H
calcium	Ca
zinc	W
tungsten	C
iron	Zn

Hint: Use a periodic table to help you.

C The earrings in the picture are made from a mixture of gold, silver, and copper.

Circle the correct **bold** words in the sentences below.

The earrings are made from **one / two / three** elements. An element **can / cannot** be broken down into other substances.

The chemical symbol for gold is **Go / Au**. The chemical symbol for silver is **Si / Ag**. The chemical symbol for copper is **Co / Cu**.

What you need to remember

An element is a substance that _____ be broken down into other substances. There are about

100 elements, which are grouped and listed in the _____ Table. Every element has its own

_____ symbol, which is a one- or two-letter code for the element. Scientists all over the world use the

same chemical _____ for the elements.

C2.2 Atoms

A The diagrams show four different substances.
Two of the substances are elements and two are not.
Each circle is one atom. The black, white, and grey atoms are different from each other.

Substance W

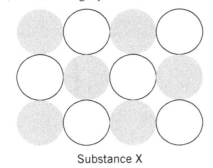
Substance X

Substance Y

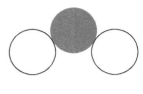
Substance Z

Write the letter of each substance in the correct column of the table.

Elements	Not elements

B Draw a line to match each sentence starter to one ending. You do not need to use all the endings.

An atom is	does not have the properties of a piece of copper.
	all the same as each other.
The atoms of copper are	the smallest part of an element that can exist.
	has the same properties as a piece of copper.
A single atom of the element copper	the same as the atoms of gold.

C The table shows data about the atoms of three elements.

Element	Radius of atom (nm)	Relative mass of atom
copper	0.128	64
mercury	0.152	201
zinc	0.133	65

Circle the correct **bold** words in the sentences below.

Of the elements in the table, copper has the atoms with the **biggest / smallest** mass. The element that has atoms with the greatest mass is **copper / mercury / zinc**. The element with the biggest atoms in the table is **copper / mercury / zinc**. Mercury is shiny, and it is liquid at room temperature. These properties are the properties of **one / many** mercury atoms.

Hint: The radius of an atom shows its size. The greater the radius, the bigger the atom.

What you need to remember

Elements are made up of _____ . An atom is the _____ part of an element that can

exist. All the _____ of an element are the same. The atoms of one element are _____

from the atoms of all the other elements. The properties of an element are the properties of _____

atoms joined together.

C2.3 Compounds

A Write one key word next to each definition. Choose from the key words in the box below.

element	compound	molecule	atom

Definition	Key word
A substance that is made of atoms of two or more elements joined together strongly.	
A substance that cannot be broken down into other substances. It is made of one type of atom.	
The smallest part of an element that can exist.	
A particle that is made up of two or more atoms strongly joined together.	

B Circle the correct **bold** words in the sentences below.

Iron is made up of one type of atom, so it is **an element / a compound**. Sulfur is also made up of one type of atom, so it is **an element / a compound**.

Iron sulfide is made up of atoms of **two / three** elements, iron and sulfur. This means that iron sulfide is **an element / a compound**. The properties of iron sulfide are **the same as / different from** the properties of iron and sulfur. This is because, in iron sulfide, iron and sulfur atoms are **joined / mixed** together to make one substance.

C The diagrams show some molecules.
The grey circles represent atoms of one element and the white circles represent atoms of another element.

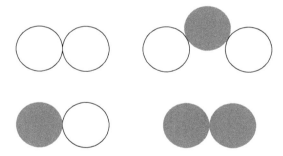

   a Use a **pencil** to draw a ring around the two molecules that represent elements.

   b Use a **pen** to draw a ring around the two molecules that represent compounds.

What you need to remember

A compound is a substance that is made up of atoms of _____ or more elements. The atoms are _____ joined together. The properties of a compound are _____ from the properties of the elements whose atoms are in it because the atoms are joined together to make _____ substance. A _____ is a group of atoms that are joined together strongly.

C2.4 Chemical formulae

A The number of different chemical symbols in a formula gives the number of elements whose atoms are in the substance.
Complete the table below.

Chemical formula of substance	Number of different elements whose atoms are in the substance
He	
CO	
H_2	
SO_3	
H_2SO_4	
NO_2	

B Draw a line to match each compound name to its chemical formula and to the elements whose atoms are in the compound.

Compound name	Chemical formula	Elements whose atoms are in the compound
magnesium oxide	CO_2	sulfur and chlorine
sodium chloride	SCl_2	magnesium and oxygen
carbon dioxide	NaCl	carbon and oxygen
sulfur dichloride	MgO	calcium, sulfur, and oxygen
calcium sulfate	$CaSO_4$	sodium and chlorine

C The diagrams show some molecules of elements and compounds.
Write the correct chemical formula next to each diagram.

 _____

 _____

 _____

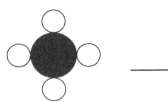 _____

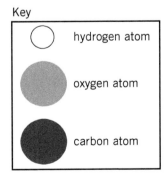

Key

hydrogen atom

oxygen atom

carbon atom

What you need to remember

A _____ formula uses chemical symbols to show the elements in a substance. It also shows

the number of atoms of one element compared to the _____ of atoms of another element. For

example, the chemical formula of water is H_2O. This shows that water is made up of two elements – hydrogen

and _____. It also shows that there are two atoms of hydrogen for every _____

atom of oxygen.

Pinchpoint question

Answer the question below, then do the follow-up activity **with the same letter** as the answer you picked.

Nitrogen dioxide is a brown gas at room temperature. It is a compound of nitrogen and oxygen. Which statement about nitrogen dioxide must be true?

A The properties of nitrogen dioxide are similar to the properties of nitrogen and oxygen.

B Nitrogen and oxygen are brown gases at room temperature.

C Nitrogen dioxide is made of atoms of two elements that are strongly joined together.

D In a jar of nitrogen dioxide, nitrogen atoms and oxygen atoms are mixed together.

Follow-up activities

A Circle the correct **bold** words and phrases in the sentences below.

The properties of a compound are **different from / similar to** the properties of the elements whose atoms are in it. For example, magnesium is a shiny silver-coloured **solid / gas** at room temperature. It burns brightly.

Oxygen is a colourless **solid / gas**. The compound made from magnesium and oxygen is **magnesium oxide / copper oxide**. This compound is a white solid at room temperature. It **does / does not** burn.

Hint: Water is a compound made from the elements hydrogen and oxygen. Are the properties of water similar to, or different from, the properties of hydrogen? For help see C1 2.3 Compounds.

B Tick the statements below that are true.

1 A compound is made up of atoms of three or more elements. ☐

2 The atoms of different elements in a compound are strongly joined together. ☐

3 Oxygen is an element in the air. It is a colourless gas at room temperature. ☐

4 The properties of nitrogen dioxide are similar to the properties of oxygen. ☐

5 The properties of a compound are different from the properties of the elements whose atoms are in it. ☐

Hint: Sodium chloride (salt) is a compound made from the elements sodium and chlorine. Chlorine is a smelly green gas at room temperature. Are the properties of sodium chloride similar to the properties of chlorine? For help see C1 2.3 Compounds.

C Complete the table to show whether each substance is an element or a compound.

Substance	Element or elements whose atoms are joined together in the substance	Is the substance an element or a compound?
chlorine	chlorine	
sulfur dioxide	sulfur and oxygen	
nitrogen monoxide	nitrogen and oxygen	
water	hydrogen and oxygen	
ozone	oxygen	
ethanol	carbon, hydrogen, and oxygen	

Hint: How many types of atom are in an element? What is the definition of a compound? For help see C1 2.3 Compounds.

D Write down **four** correct sentences from the sentence starters and endings below.

| A compound is a substance that is | strongly joined together. |

| The atoms of the different elements in a compound are | strongly joined together. |

| In sulfur dioxide, atoms of sulfur and oxygen are | made up of atoms of two or more elements. |

| Sulfur dioxide is | made up of atoms of two elements. |

_____

_____

_____

_____

Hint: In a compound, atoms of different elements are not just mixed together. For help see C1 2.3 Compounds.

 Pinchpoint review
Now look back at the question – do you think you chose the right letter?
Turn to the Answers page to find out.

C3.1 Chemical reactions

A Sam burns wood in a bonfire. Burning wood involves chemical reactions.
Complete the sentences to describe some signs of chemical reactions. Use the words in the box below.

feels	hears	smells	sees

Sam _____ flames.

Sam _____ smoke.

Sam _____ heat from the bonfire.

Sam _____ loud 'pops' as the wood burns.

B Draw a line to show whether each chemical change is useful or not useful.

making a medicine

useful

breakfast cereal going stale

not useful

a car going rusty

a tree making wood

C Tick the statements about chemical reactions below that are true.

1 A chemical reaction makes new substances. ☐

2 The substances at the start of a chemical reaction are the same as the substances at the end. ☐

3 In every chemical reaction, energy is transferred to the surroundings. ☐

4 In a chemical reaction, the atoms are joined together in one way before the reaction and in a different way after the reaction. ☐

5 It is easy to reverse a chemical reaction to get the starting substances back again. ☐

6 A catalyst is a substance that speeds up a reaction, and is used up in the process. ☐

D Draw a line to complete each statement. You can use each ending once or more than once.

Melting is an example of

It is easy to get back the starting substances in

a physical change.

New substances are made in

a chemical change.

Dissolving is an example of

What you need to remember

A chemical reaction is a change that makes _____ substances. In a chemical reaction, the atoms in

the starting substances are _____ and join together _____. It is _____

easy to reverse a chemical reaction. Chemical reactions involve _____ transfers to or from the

surroundings. Chemists use _____ to speed up reactions. Not all changes involve chemical reactions.

A _____ change, such as melting, is usually reversible.

C3.2 Word equations

A Carbon reacts with oxygen to make carbon dioxide.

Circle the correct **bold** words in the sentences below.

Carbon is one of the **reactants / products** in the reaction. Oxygen is the other **reactant / product**. Carbon dioxide is the **reactant / product** of the reaction.

In this reaction, two **elements / compounds** have reacted together to make one **element / compound**.

B In the word equations below, circle each **reactant in pencil** and each **product in pen**.

   a iron + sulfur $\rightarrow$ iron sulfide

   b methane + oxygen $\rightarrow$ carbon dioxide + water

   c copper carbonate $\rightarrow$ copper oxide + carbon dioxide

C Write a word equation for each reaction below.

   a Sodium and chlorine react together to make sodium chloride.

   _____

   b Aluminium reacts with iodine to make aluminium iodide.

   _____

   c Propane burns in oxygen to make carbon dioxide and water.

   _____

D The diagram below shows some atoms in the reaction of hydrogen with oxygen to make water. Label the diagram using the labels in the box.

reactant molecules	**oxygen molecule**	**product molecules**

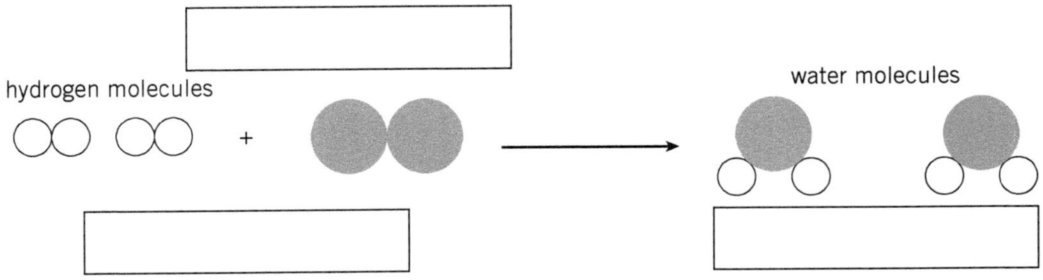

hydrogen molecules

water molecules

What you need to remember

The starting substances in a chemical reaction are called _____. The substances that are made in a chemical reaction are called _____. In a word equation, the reactants are on the _____ of the arrow and the products are on the _____ of the arrow. The _____ means 'reacts to make'.

C3.3 Burning fuels

A Draw a line to match each word to its definition.

fuel	any reaction in which a substance reacts with oxygen
combustion	a material that burns to transfer energy by heating
oxidation	the scientific word for burning
rusting	an oxidation reaction that is not useful

B The products of a combustion reaction are the substances that are made when a substance burns. Complete the table with the names of the products of combustion.

Fuel	Product or products of combustion
carbon	
hydrogen	
butane (a compound of carbon and hydrogen that is used in camping stoves)	

C Riley does an investigation to compare the increase in temperature of water when two different fuels burn. Here is a diagram of the apparatus. The fuels are wax and ethanol.

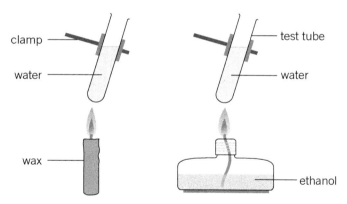

The list below shows the variables in the investigation.
Circle the independent variable. Draw a **box** around the dependent variable. **Underline** the **two** control variables.

volume of water   fuel

increase in temperature of water   distance of flame from test tube

---

What you need to remember

A fuel is a material that burns to transfer _____ by heating. The scientific word for burning is

_____ . When a fuel burns it reacts with _____ from the air. The product of combustion

of carbon is _____ . The products of combustion of a compound that is made

from carbon and hydrogen atoms are carbon dioxide and _____ . Burning reactions are oxidation

reactions. In oxidation reactions, substances react with _____ .

C3.4 Thermal decomposition

A Tick the statements below that are **true**.

1. In a decomposition reaction, a compound breaks down. ☐
2. Every decomposition reaction has two or more products. ☐
3. The products of a decomposition reaction are always elements. ☐
4. In a decomposition reaction, there is one reactant only. ☐

B Raj heats copper carbonate in the apparatus shown in the diagram.

clamp
metal carbonate
limewater
Bunsen burner

He writes the time for the limewater to start looking cloudy in the table below.

He then repeats the experiment with two more compounds.

Compound	Time for limewater to start looking cloudy (minutes)
copper carbonate	1
potassium carbonate	did not go cloudy after heating for 10 minutes
lead carbonate	4

Draw a line to match each compound with the correct statement about its decomposition. Use the information in the table to help you.

copper carbonate		did not decompose

lead carbonate		decomposed most quickly

potassium carbonate		decomposed more slowly than copper carbonate

C Highlight or underline the **two** word equations that show decomposition reactions.

W calcium carbonate $\longrightarrow$ calcium oxide + carbon dioxide
X magnesium + nitrogen $\longrightarrow$ magnesium nitride
Y methane + oxygen $\longrightarrow$ carbon dioxide + water
Z sodium nitrate $\longrightarrow$ sodium nitrite + oxygen

What you need to remember

In a decomposition reaction, _____ reactant breaks down to make _____ or more

products. The reactant must be a _____ . The products can be elements or _____ .

Zinc carbonate, for example, decomposes to make zinc _____ and _____

_____ . When heat is needed to make a substance break down, the reaction is called a

_____ decomposition reaction.

C3.5 Conservation of mass

A Circle the correct **bold** words and phrases in the sentences below.

In a chemical reaction, the total mass of the reactants is **equal to / greater than** the total mass of the products.

In a physical change, such as **melting / burning**, the total mass **increases / does not change**. This is the law of **combustion / conservation** of mass.

B The statements below describe how to weigh out 10 g of salt. They are in the wrong order. Read the statements and write down the correct order.

Correct order ☐ ☐ ☐ ☐

1 Press the tare button on the balance.

2 Use a spatula to put some salt on the watch glass.

3 Place a watch glass on a balance.

4 Add more and more salt until the reading on the balance is 10 g.

C Anna finds the mass of some magnesium. Then she sets up the apparatus shown.
She lights the Bunsen burner and heats the crucible, opening the lid every now and again.

She stops heating and waits for everything to cool.

Then she finds the mass of the product. Her results are in the table.

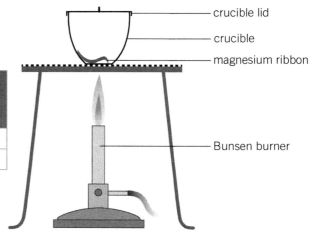

crucible lid
crucible
magnesium ribbon
Bunsen burner

Substance	Is this substance a reactant or product?	Mass of substance (g)
magnesium	reactant	0.12
magnesium oxide	product	0.20

The word equation for the reaction is
        magnesium + oxygen ⟶ magnesium oxide

Circle the correct **bold** words and phrases in the sentences below.

In Anna's experiment, the solid reactant is **magnesium / magnesium oxide**, of mass 0.12 g. The product is

magnesium / magnesium oxide, of mass 0.20 g. The mass of solid has **decreased / increased**. This means that

magnesium reacts with a **gas / solid** from the air – oxygen. The total mass of the two reactants, magnesium and

oxygen, is **the same as / less than** the mass of the product, magnesium oxide. This means that the mass of oxygen

that reacts is 0.20 g – 0.12 g = **0.32 g / 0.08 g**.

What you need to remember

In a chemical reaction or in a _____ change, the total mass does not change. This means that in a

chemical reaction, the total mass of reactants is equal to the total mass of _____. This is the law of

_____ of mass. Balanced symbol equations show the relative amounts of _____ and

products.

C3.6 Exothermic and endothermic

A Complete each sentence about reactions by drawing a line to match the sentence starter with the correct ending.

| A chemical reaction | | transfers energy from the surroundings to the reaction mixture. |

| An exothermic reaction | | involves energy transfers. |

| An endothermic reaction | | transfers energy from the reaction mixture to the surroundings. |

B Barney sets up the apparatus opposite.

He pours dilute hydrochloric acid into the cup, and measures its temperature.

Then he adds a piece of magnesium ribbon. There is a chemical reaction.

At the end of the chemical reaction he measures the temperature again.

Then Barney repeats the experiment with zinc instead of magnesium.

Some of his results are in the table. Complete the table by filling in the empty boxes.

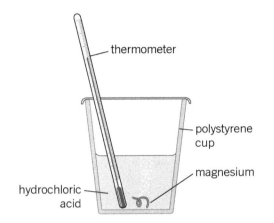

thermometer

polystyrene cup

magnesium

hydrochloric acid

Reacting substances	Temperature before the reaction (°C)	Temperature after the reaction (°C)	Temperature change (°C)
hydrochloric acid and magnesium	20	28	
hydrochloric acid and zinc	20		5

C The sentences below are about Barney's experiment in activity **B**.

Circle the correct **bold** words.

The temperatures of both reacting mixtures **decrease / increase** at first. This means that the reactions are **exothermic / endothermic**. The temperature change for the reaction with magnesium is **less / more** than the temperature change for the reaction with zinc. This means that the reaction with magnesium is **less / more** exothermic.

Pinchpoint question

Answer the question below, then do the follow-up activity **with the same letter** as the answer you picked.

The gas used as fuel in a gas hob consists primarily of methane.

What does this word equation show?

methane + oxygen ⟶ carbon dioxide + water

A Methane and oxygen react together to make carbon dioxide and water.

B The reactants in the reaction are carbon dioxide and water.

C The reactants in the reaction are methane and carbon dioxide.

D Methane and oxygen are the same as carbon dioxide and water.

Follow-up activities

A Write a word equation for each reaction below.

a Hydrogen reacts with oxygen to make water.

_____

b Iron reacts with chlorine to make iron chloride.

_____

c Butane and oxygen react together to make carbon dioxide and water.

_____

d On heating, copper carbonate breaks down to make copper oxide and carbon dioxide.

_____

Hint: Remember to write down the names of the starting substances (reactants) first, on the left of the arrow. See C1 3.2 for help.

B In the word equations below, **circle each reactant** and **underline each product**.

a sulfur   +   oxygen   ⟶   sulfur dioxide

b aluminium   +   chlorine   ⟶   aluminium chloride

c ethane   +   oxygen   ⟶   carbon dioxide   +   water

d zinc carbonate   ⟶   zinc oxide   +   carbon dioxide

Hint: Which side of the arrow are the reactants? See C1 3.2 for help.

C Write down **five** correct sentences about word equations from the sentence starters and endings below. You may use one starter and one ending more than once to make the fifth sentence.

| The reactants are | shown on the right of the arrow. |

| The products are | reacts to make. |

| The arrow means | shown on the left of the arrow. |

| The equation shows that ethane and oxygen react together to make | carbon dioxide and water. |

_____

_____

_____

_____

_____

Hint: Reactants are the starting substances in a chemical reaction. See C1 3.2 for help.

D The diagrams show the atoms in the reactants and products of a chemical reaction.

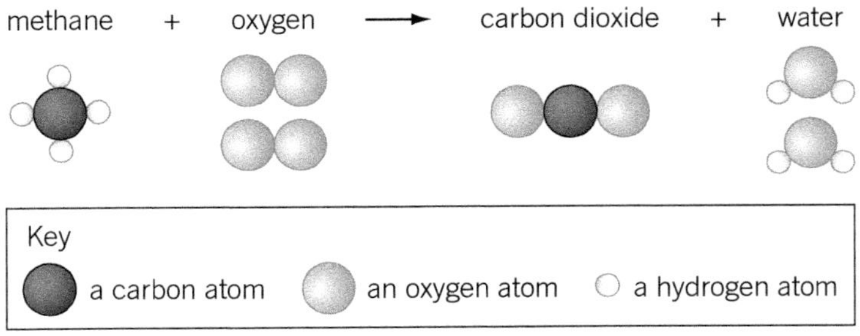

methane + oxygen ⟶ carbon dioxide + water

Key
● a carbon atom   ○ an oxygen atom   ○ a hydrogen atom

Tick the statements about the chemical reaction that are **true**.

1 There are four oxygen atoms on the left of the arrow and two on the right. ☐

2 There are the same number of carbon atoms on each side of the arrow. ☐

3 The atoms are joined together in different arrangements on each side of the arrow. ☐

4 The substances on the left of the arrow are the same as the substances on the right of the arrow. ☐

Hint: Atoms are joined together differently in every different substance. See C1 3.2 for help.

C4.1 Acids and alkalis

A Draw a line to correctly complete each sentence.

Lemon juice is an

Toothpaste is an

If something feels soapy it is likely to be an

If something tastes sour it is likely to be an

alkali.

acid.

B This hazard symbol is displayed on bottles that contain some acids and alkalis.

Complete the table by writing each phrase in the box below in the correct column.

burning your skin   damaging your eyes   wear safety glasses   wear gloves

Risk from this hazard	How to control this risk

C Ms Khan has two bottles of sulfuric acid, **X** and **Y**. There is one litre of acid in each bottle.

- The acid in bottle **X** is concentrated.
- The acid in bottle **Y** is dilute.

Circle the correct **bold** words in the sentences below.

There is more water in bottle **X / Y**. There are more acid particles in bottle **X / Y**.

The acid in bottle **X / Y** is more damaging to eyes and skin. Ms Khan could make the acid in bottle X less concentrated by adding **water / acid** to it.

What you need to remember

Do **not** taste or feel substances in science unless your teacher tells you to. Acids taste _____ and alkalis feel _____. Wear safety glasses or safety goggles when working with acids and alkalis because many of these substances are _____. This means that they burn eyes and _____. A concentrated solution of alkali has more alkali particles in it than a _____ solution.

C4.2 Indicators and pH

A Universal indicator gives different colours in acids, alkalis, and neutral solutions.

Draw a line to match each type of solution with its colour in universal indicator.

acid		blue or purple

alkali		red or orange or yellow

neutral		green

B The statements below can be reordered to correctly describe the method for identifying whether a solution is acidic, alkaline, or neutral.

Write the order of the statements that gives the best method.

Correct order ☐ ☐ ☐ ☐ ☐ ☐

1   Add a few drops of universal indicator.

2   Shake the test tube and its contents carefully.

3   Pour about 1 cm³ of the substance into a test tube.

4   Put on your eye protection.

5   Put a bung into the test tube.

6   Compare the colour of the mixture to the colours on the indicator chart.

C The pH scale measures acidity and alkalinity.

Complete the table to show the pH of acidic, alkaline, and neutral solutions.

pH	Is a solution with this pH acidic, alkaline, or neutral?
less than 7	
exactly 7	
more than 7	

D Colour the pH scale below to show the colour of universal indicator at each pH.

pH	1	2	3	4	5	6	7	8	9	10	11	12	13	14
colour														

What you need to remember

Indicators show whether a solution is acidic, alkaline, or _____. Universal indicator is

_____ or orange or yellow in acids, green in _____ solutions, and blue or purple in

_____ solutions. The _____ scale measures how acidic or alkaline a solution is. The

pH of an acid is _____ than 7. The pH of a _____ solution is 7. The pH of an alkali is

_____ than 7.

C4.3 Neutralisation

A Draw a line to match each word to its definition.

| base | | a substance that neutralises an acid |

| alkali | | when an acid reacts with a substance that cancels it out |

| neutralisation | | a soluble base |

B Highlight or underline the **two** neutralisation reactions in the list below.
- Burning magnesium in air.
- Adding a base to a lake with acidic water.
- Adding an acid to soil of pH 9.
- Heating copper carbonate to make copper oxide and carbon dioxide.

C Ash investigates three different types of indigestion tablets.

He measures the volume of acid that each tablet can neutralise.

He uses the same type and concentration of acid each time.

He does each experiment at the same temperature.

Complete the table to show the different types of variable. Use the words in the box below.

| control | independent | dependent |

Variable	Type of variable
volume of acid that the tablet neutralises	
temperature	
type of tablet	
type of acid	
concentration of acid	

D Sarah uses the equipment shown, as well as some other things, to do an experiment.

Circle the correct **bold** words in the sentences below.

Sarah pours some acid into a **test tube / beaker**. She dips **indicator / filter** paper into the acid. The pH is **2 / 12**. Then she uses a **spatula / test tube** to add copper oxide to the acid. She stirs the mixture with a **stirring rod / spatula**.

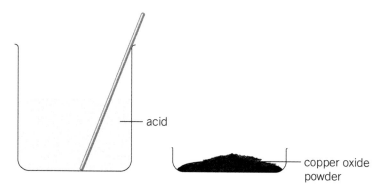

acid

copper oxide powder

Then Sarah dips indicator paper into the mixture. The pH is **5 / 1**. The pH has **decreased / increased** because copper oxide is a base. Copper oxide has **neutralised / combusted** some of the acid.

What you need to remember

When a base reacts with an acid the acid is _____ by the base. If you add a base to an acid the pH _____. If you add an acid to a base, the pH _____.

Making salts

A Tick the statements below that are **true**.

1 When an acid reacts with a metal, one of the products is a salt. ☐

2 When an acid reacts with a base, one of the products is a salt. ☐

3 When an acid reacts to make a salt, hydrogen atoms replace the metal atoms that were in the acid. ☐

B Draw a line to match each acid to the type of salt it makes.

| hydrochloric acid | | nitrates |

| sulfuric acid | | sulfates |

| nitric acid | | chlorides |

C In the three sentences below, circle in **pencil** the names of the reactants and circle in **pen** the name of the product that is a salt.

a Magnesium reacts with hydrochloric acid to make magnesium chloride and hydrogen.

b Zinc oxide reacts with sulfuric acid to make zinc sulfate and water.

c Copper oxide reacts with hydrochloric acid to make copper chloride and water.

D Complete the word equations for each of the reactions described in activity **C**.

a magnesium + hydrochloric acid ➔ _____ _____ + hydrogen

b zinc oxide + sulfuric acid ➔ _____ _____ + _____

c copper oxide + hydrochloric acid ➔ _____ _____ + water

E This apparatus is used to remove water from a salt solution.

a Label the diagram using the labels provided in the box below.

| evaporating basin   salt solution |
| beaker   boiling water |

b Complete the sentence below.

A salt is a c_____ that forms when an

a_____ reacts with a m_____

element, or a c_____ that includes a metal.

What you need to remember

When an acid reacts with a metal or a base, one of the products is a _____. Hydrochloric acid makes

_____ salts. Sulfuric acid makes _____ salts. When an acid reacts to make a salt, metal

atoms replace the _____ atoms that were in the acid.

Pinchpoint question

Answer the question below, then do the follow-up activity **with the same letter** as the answer you picked.

Tom measures the pH of three solutions. His results are shown in the diagram.

Which is the best conclusion?

A   Solution Z is more acidic than solutions X and Y.

B   Solutions X and Y are acidic and solution Z is alkaline.

C   Solutions X and Y are equally acidic, and solution Z is neutral.

D   Solution X is more acidic than solution Y, and solution Z is neutral.

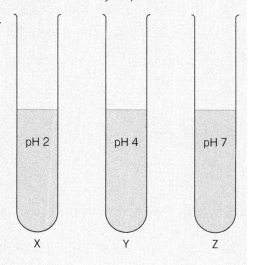

Follow-up activities

A   Sophie measures the pH of five solutions. Write down the letters of the solutions in order of **increasing** acidity.

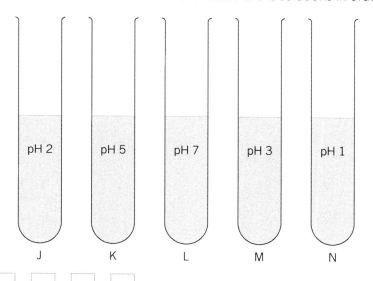

Correct order: ☐ ☐ ☐ ☐ ☐

Hint: What happens to the pH as acidity increases? For help see C1 4.2 Indicators and pH.

B   Circle the correct **bold** words in the sentences below.

The pH of a solution tells you how acidic or alkaline the solution is. If the pH is below 7 the solution is **acidic / alkaline**. The lower the pH, the **more / less** acidic the solution. If the pH is 7 the solution is neutral. If the pH is greater than 7 the solution is **acidic / alkaline**. The **lower / higher** the pH the more alkaline the solution.

Hint: An alkaline solution has a pH greater than 7. What do you know about the pH of acidic solutions? For help see C1 4.2 Indicators and pH.

C The diagram below shows the pH scale.

Write one letter, **V–Z**, in each box below the scale to label the pH scale correctly.

V	a slightly acidic solution
W	a slightly alkaline solution
X	a neutral solution
Y	a very acidic solution
Z	a very alkaline solution

1	2	3	4	5	6	7	8	9	10	11	12	13	14

Hint: What happens to the pH as acidity increases? What happens to the pH as solutions become more alkaline? For help see C1 4.2 Indicators and pH.

D Tick the statements below that are **true**.

1 The lower the pH, the less acidic the solution. ☐

2 If you add alkali to a solution of pH 2, the pH increases. ☐

3 The lower the pH, the more alkaline the solution. ☐

4 If you add acid to a solution of pH 12, its pH increases. ☐

5 A solution of pH 3 is more acidic than a solution of pH 5. ☐

6 A solution of pH 10 is less alkaline than a solution of pH 12. ☐

7 A solution of pH 6 is more acidic than a solution of pH 2. ☐

8 A neutral solution has a pH between 6 and 8. ☐

Hint: What happens to pH as alkalinity increases? For help see C1 4.2 Indicators and pH.

Pinchpoint review

Now look back at the question – do you think you chose the right letter?

Turn to the Answers page to find out.

C1 Revision questions

1 ⚗ Draw a line from each statement to the correct particle diagram. **(4 marks)**

| The substance is a liquid. |
| The particles are vibrating on the spot. |
| You cannot pour the substance. |
| The substance condenses to make a liquid. |

2 ⚗ A student does three experiments – **A**, **B**, and **C**.

He writes down his observations.

Experiment	What we did	Observation
A	Charice put perfume on her wrist.	After 5 minutes we could smell perfume from the other side of the room.
B	We pumped up a balloon.	The balloon burst.
C	We put some water in a freezer.	After 30 minutes the water had turned to ice.

a Which experiment shows diffusion?
Tick **one** box. **(1 mark)**

A ☐ B ☐ C ☐

b Which experiment shows a change of state?
Tick **one** box. **(1 mark)**

A ☐ B ☐ C ☐

c Which experiment shows gas pressure?
Tick **one** box. **(1 mark)**

A ☐ B ☐ C ☐

3 ⚗ What are the starting substances called in **every** chemical reaction?

Tick **one** box. **(1 mark)**

elements ☐   reactants ☐

products ☐   compounds ☐

4 ⚗ Which statements about chemical reactions are **always** true?

Tick **two** statements. **(2 marks)**

New substances are made. ☐

Energy is transferred to the surroundings. ☐

Atoms are rearranged and join together differently. ☐

The products are compounds. ☐

5 ⚗⚗ Draw a line from each word to its definition.

(4 marks)

| atom |
| base |
| compound |
| fuel |

| a substance made up of atoms of two or more elements, strongly joined together |
| the smallest particle of an element that can exist |
| a substance that burns to transfer energy by heating |
| a substance that neutralises an acid |

6 ⚗⚗ Draw a line to match each pH value to its description. **(4 marks)**

| 1 |
| 6 |
| 7 |
| 14 |

| a very alkaline solution |
| a neutral solution |
| a slightly acidic solution |
| a very acidic solution |

7 Compare the arrangement and movement of the particles of a substance as a solid and as a liquid and explain how these affect the properties of both states. **(6 marks)**

_____

_____

_____

_____

_____

_____

_____

_____

8 A student sets up the apparatus in **Figure 1**.

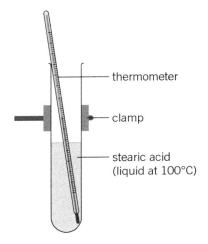

thermometer

clamp

stearic acid
(liquid at 100°C)

Figure 1

She measures the temperature every minute as the stearic acid cools down.

She writes her results in **Table 1**.

Table 1

Time (min)	Temperature (°C)
0	100
1	90
2	80
3	70
4	70
5	70
6	70
7	60
8	50
9	40

a Plot the results on the graph axes, showing each point as a cross, x. **(2 marks)**

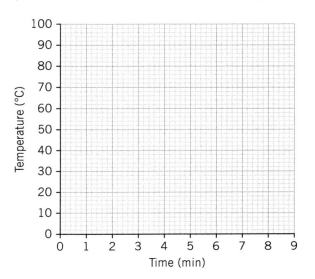

b Write down the temperature at which a change of state occurs. **(1 mark)**

_____ °C

c Write down the state of the stearic acid at 90 °C. **(1 mark)**

_____

d Write down the state of the stearic acid at 40 °C. **(1 mark)**

_____

9 A teacher mixes two elements – aluminium and iodine. He adds a drop of water, and the students see bright white flames. In the chemical reaction, the elements make a compound, aluminium iodide. A student writes down some of his observations in **Table 2**.

Table 2

Substance	Appearance
aluminium	shiny silver-coloured powder
iodine	grey crystals
aluminium iodide	white powder

a What is the chemical symbol of aluminium? Tick **one** box. **(1 mark)**

AL ☐   **al** ☐   **aL** ☐   **Al** ☐

b Define the term 'element'. **(2 marks)**

_____

_____

69

c Write down one conclusion that the student could make about elements and compounds from the information in **Table 2**. (**1 mark**)

_____

_____

d Write down **two** pieces of evidence that show that a chemical reaction has occurred. (**2 marks**)

1 _____

2 _____

10 ⚗️⚗️ The diagrams show molecules of some elements and compounds. Draw a line from each diagram to the correct formula. (**4 marks**)

Key

⊘ = nitrogen atom

⬤ = oxygen atom

⊘⊘	NO$_2$
⊘⬤	NO
⊘⬤⬤	N$_2$
⬤⬤⬤	N$_2$O
	O$_3$

11 ⚗️⚗️ A compound has the formula SiO$_2$.

a Write down the number of oxygen atoms that are in the compound for every one silicon atom. (**1 mark**)

_____

b Write down the number of oxygen atoms that are in the compound for every 10 silicon atoms. (**1 mark**)

_____

12 ⚗️⚗️ Substance **X** has the formula O$_2$. Substance **Y** has the formula SO$_2$.
Compare substances **X** and **Y** in terms of:

• type of substance

• number of atoms. (**4 marks**)

_____

_____

_____

_____

_____

_____

_____

13 ⚗️⚗️ A student makes copper chloride crystals from dilute hydrochloric acid and copper oxide powder. This is the method used.

Step 1 Add copper oxide powder to dilute hydrochloric acid. Stop adding when some copper oxide powder is left over.

Step 2 Filter the mixture.

Step 3 Pour the copper chloride solution into an evaporating basin.

Step 4 Heat until all the water has evaporated.

a Complete the word equation for the reaction. (**1 mark**)

hydrochloric acid + _____ _____ ⟶
copper chloride + water

b Name the two products of the reaction. (**2 marks**)

_____ and _____

c Suggest one improvement to step 1 to make sure as much as possible of the copper oxide reacts. (**1 mark**)

_____

d Name the substance left in the filter paper in step 2. (**1 mark**)

_____

e Suggest one improvement to step 4 to make the crystals as big as possible. **(1 mark)**

_____

_____

f Write down **two** safety precautions the students should take in step 4. **(2 marks)**

1 _____

2 _____

14 🏺🏺 Here are four word equations.

W magnesium + oxygen ⟶ magnesium oxide

X ice ⟶ liquid water

Y magnesium carbonate ⟶ magnesium oxide + carbon dioxide

Z hydrogen peroxide ⟶ water + oxygen

a Write down the letter of the **one** equation that shows a change of state. **(1 mark)**

_____

b Write down the letter of the **one** equation that shows two elements joining together. **(1 mark)**

_____

c Write down the letters of **two** equations that show decomposition reactions. **(2 marks)**

_____ and _____

d Write down the letter of the **one** equation that shows an exothermic reaction. **(1 mark)**

_____

e Write down the letter of the **one** equation that shows a combustion reaction. **(1 mark)**

_____

15 🏺🏺 A teacher heats up some iron. She places it in a jar of bromine gas.

The reacting mixture of iron and bromine glows bright red.

At the end, there is a brown powder in the jar. This is iron bromide.

The word equation for the reaction is

iron + bromine ⟶ iron bromide

a Describe one piece of evidence that shows there is a chemical reaction. **(1 mark)**

_____

b The teacher started with 1 g of iron. The mass of iron bromide at the end was 5.3 g.

Calculate the mass of bromine that reacted with the iron.

Show how you worked out your answer. **(2 marks)**

mass of bromine = _____ g

16 🏺🏺 **Table 3** shows the masses of the atoms of three mystery elements, labelled **X**, **Y**, and **Z**.

Table 3

Element	Relative mass of atom	Radius of atom (nm)
X	178	0.16
Y	24	0.16
Z	91	0.16

a Write down the **letter** of the element whose atoms have the greatest mass. **(1 mark)**

_____

b Write down the **letter** of the element whose atoms have the smallest mass. **(1 mark)**

_____

c Compare the size of an atom of **Z** to an atom of **Y**. **(1 mark)**

_____

d A 1 cm³ cube of **Z** has a greater mass than a 1 cm³ cube of **Y**.

Use data in the table to suggest a reason for this observation. **(2 marks)**

_____

_____

e Predict which has the greater mass, a 1 cm³ cube of **X** or a 1 cm³ cube of **Z**.

Give a reason for your answer. **(3 marks)**

_____

_____

_____

C1 Checklist

Revision question number	Outcome	Topic reference	☹	😐	☺
1	Match particle models to the properties of a material.	C1.1			
2a	Describe examples of diffusion.	C1.6			
2b	Describe how substances change as the temperature changes.	C1.3			
2c	State examples of gas pressure in everyday situations.	C1.7			
3	State what a reactant is.	C3.1			
4	State what a chemical reaction is.	C3.1			
	State what happens to the reactants in a chemical reaction.				
5	State what atoms are.	C2.2			
	State what a base is.	C4.3			
	State what a compound is.	C2.3			
	State what a fuel is.	C3.3			
6	Interpret pH values.	C4.2			
7	Describe the arrangement and movement of particles in substances in different states.	C1.2			
	Use ideas about particles to explain the properties of a substance in its three states.				
8a	Add data to a graph or chart.	WS1.3			
8b, c, d	Use cooling data to decide the melting point of stearic acid.	C1.3			
9a	Recall chemical symbols.	C2.1			
9b	State what an element is.	C2.1			
9c	State that a compound has different properties from the elements whose atoms are in it.	C2.3			
9d	State some signs of a chemical reaction.	C3.1			
10	Write and interpret chemical formulae.	C2.4			
11a, b	Write and interpret chemical formulae.	C2.4			
12	Write and interpret chemical formulae.	C2.4			
13a	Write word equations to represent chemical reactions.	C3.2			
13b	Identify reactants and products for a given reaction.	C3.2			
13c, d, e	Use practical techniques to make a salt.	C4.4			
13f	Suggest how to carry out a practical safely.	WS1.2			
14a	Identify changes of state.	C1.3			
14b	Identify reactants and products in word equations.	C3.2			
14c	Identify decomposition reactions from word equations.	C3.4			
14d	Identify a reaction as endothermic or exothermic.	C3.6			
14e	Identify combustion reactions from word equations.	C3.3			
15a	State some signs of a chemical reaction.	C3.1			
15b	Calculate masses of reactants and products.	C3.5 🔢			
16a, b, c	Present some simple facts about an element.	C2.1			
16d, e	Use data on atoms to predict properties of substances.	C2.2 🔢			

P1.1 Introduction to forces

A Circle the force represented by the arrow for this falling ball.

friction	air resistance	force of gravity

B What is the force displayed on the newtonmeter below? _____

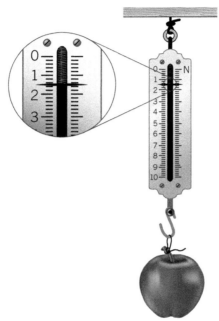

C Draw a line to match each sentence's start to a correct middle and ending.

A force of friction		of the Earth on the water		helps a skydiver land safely.

A force of air resistance		of the road on the tyre		makes spilt water spread into a puddle.

A force of gravity		of the air on their parachute		makes a bus change speed.

D A person is standing on the ground. Think about the forces acting on them.

Circle the correct **bold** words in these sentences to describe these forces.

The force of the Earth on the person is due to **support / gravity**.

The force that makes up an interaction pair with this one is the force of the **Earth / person** on the **Earth / person**.

What you need to remember

A force can be a _____ or a _____. Forces explain why objects _____

in the way that they do. They can change the _____ that objects are moving in, and change their

_____. They might be a non-contact force, such as _____, or a contact force, such as

_____ or _____. Forces always come in pairs, called _____ pairs. Forces

can be _____ with a newtonmeter. All forces are measured in _____.

P1.2 Squashing and stretching

A Complete these sentences about the effects of forces on objects. You can choose from the following words:

supports	**stretch**	**deforms**	**compress**

When a falling ball hits the floor, the ball _____. Forces can

_____ (squash) or _____ objects.

B The statements below can be reordered to explain how solid surfaces provide a support force. Read the statements and write down the order of statements that you think will give the best explanation.

Correct order ☐ ☐ ☐ ☐

1 Your weight pushes the particles in the floor together.

2 The Earth pulls down on you with a force of gravity, your weight.

3 The bonds push back and support you.

4 The bonds between the particles in the floor are compressed.

C A spring obeys Hooke's Law. It stretches by 5 cm when a force of 20 N is applied to it.

Predict how far it will stretch if a force of 40 N is applied to it. _____ cm

D On the graph paper on page 80, plot a graph of extension (y-axis) against force (x-axis) using the data in the table. Label the axes, and draw a line of best fit.

Force (N)	Extension (cm)
1.0	0.5
2.0	1.0
3.0	1.4
4.0	1.8
5.0	2.3
6.0	2.9
7.0	3.3
8.0	3.7

Does the graph you have drawn obey Hooke's Law?
Circle your answer. **Yes / No**

Give a reason for your answer: _____

_____

_____

_____

What you need to remember

Forces can change the shape of objects, or _____ them. Forces can _____ (squash) or

stretch objects. When you stand on the floor, your weight compresses the bonds between the particles in the floor.

They push back and the floor _____ up on you when you stand on it. This support force from the floor

is called the _____ force. Bungee cords, springs, and even lift cables all _____ when you

exert a force on them. The amount that they stretch is called the _____. A bungee cord will pull back

on the person with a force called _____. Springs are special: if you double the force on a spring, the

extension will _____. This relationship is called _____ and it is a

_____ relationship. At some point the spring will not go back to its original length when you remove

the force. This is the _____ limit.

P1.3 Drag forces and friction

A Draw a line to match each force with its cause and an example.

Force	Cause	Example
water resistance	rough surfaces are touching	a dolphin swimming
air resistance	must push many liquid particles out of the way	brakes on a bus
friction	must push many gas particles out of the way	a bird flying

B Complete the table to describe the role of friction or drag forces in each situation.

Situation	Role of friction or drag forces
A boat when its engine stops.	
A mechanic putting oil on a bicycle chain.	
Walking forwards on a pavement.	
A skydiver opening her parachute.	

C A student has planned an experiment to investigate friction, but has made two mistakes. Read his plan below, and identify his **two** mistakes and suggest how to correct them.

> I will pull an object across a surface and measure the force required using a pulley.
> I will then repeat the experiment using a different surface and a different speed.

Mistake	Correction

What you need to remember

_____ grips objects because, although their surfaces might look smooth, they are actually

_____ . One way to reduce friction is to use _____ . Drag forces, such as

_____ resistance or _____ resistance, happen because an object has to push air or

water molecules out of the way. Making an object more _____ is a way to reduce drag. If no other

force is applied, friction and drag forces cause an object to _____ _____ or stop.

P1.4 Forces at a distance

A Complete the table by ticking whether the forces act at a distance or are a contact force.

Force	✓ acts at a distance	✓ contact force
water resistance		
magnetic		
friction		
gravitational		
air resistance		

B Complete the following sentences using these keywords:

weight	newton	kilogram	mass

A _____ is a unit of force. The force of gravity on an object is called its _____.

A _____ is a unit of mass. The amount of 'stuff' something is made of is called its _____.

C Circle the correct **bold** phrases in the sentences below.

A field is a region where something experiences **an acceleration / friction / a force**. Around the Earth there is a gravitational field where **magnets / masses / electrical charges** experience a force due to gravity. As an object gets further from the Earth, the field **stays the same / gets stronger / gets weaker**, so that the force on the object becomes smaller.

D Weight can be calculated using the formula:

weight (N) = mass (kg) x gravitational field strength, g (N/kg)

A dog has a mass of 20 kg. Calculate its weight: _____ N.

Hint: On Earth gravitational field strength is about 10 N/kg.

E The table shows the strength of the gravitational field in different places. A value of 1 N/kg means that a mass of 1 kg experiences a gravitational force (a weight) of 1 N. An astronaut and her equipment have a mass of 160 kg. Complete the table by calculating the weight of the astronaut in each place.

Place	Gravitational field strength (N/kg)	Weight of astronaut and her equipment (N)
the Earth's surface	9.8	
in orbit around the Earth	8.7	
the Moon's surface	1.6	
far from any star or planet	0.0	

What you need to remember

_____ are regions where an object experiences a _____ force, such as gravitational, magnetic, or electrostatic forces. For instance, around a _____ there is an electrostatic field. If another _____ comes into that field, it experiences a force, and the force gets _____ the closer it comes.

Every object exerts a _____ force on every other object. It increases with mass and _____ with distance. Weight is the force of _____ on an object. You can calculate weight using the equation:

weight (N) = _____ (kg) x gravitational field strength, g (N/kg)

P1.5 Balanced and unbalanced

A Circle the correct **bold** words in the sentences below.

When someone is standing still, the forces on them are **balanced / unbalanced**: the downwards force on the

person due to **friction / gravity** from the Earth is **equal to / greater than** the upwards **gravity / support force**

from the floor and there are no **horizontal / vertical** forces acting.

B Think about a cyclist who is speeding up, away from some traffic lights.

    a Write a sentence comparing the sizes of the forward and backward forces on them.

    _____

    b Are the forces balanced or unbalanced? _____

    c Is the cyclist in equilibrium? _____

C Here is a diagram of the cyclist in activity **B**. Complete it with labelled arrows to show the forward force due to the
road pushing on the tyres with friction, and the backward force due to air resistance.

D A while later, the horizontal forces on the cyclist are as shown below.

Describe their likely motion.

_____

Pinchpoint question

Answer the question below, then do the follow-up activity **with the same letter** as the answer you picked.

Here is a diagram of the horizontal force acting on a bus. Which of the following statements is correct?

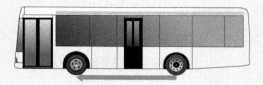

A   The bus is changing speed.

B   The bus is stationary and will remain stationary.

C   The forces on the bus are balanced.

D   Forces always occur in pairs, so the diagram for the bus is wrong.

Follow-up activities

A   Add at least one force arrow to each diagram below to cause the predicted motion. All of the cars are driving up the page.

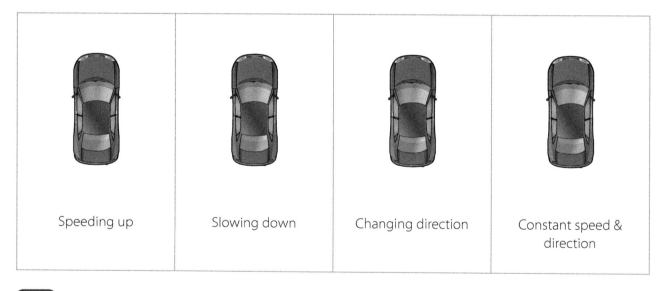

| Speeding up | Slowing down | Changing direction | Constant speed & direction |

Hint: Which direction must an unbalanced force be to cause each change? For help see P1 1.5 Balanced and unbalanced.

B   Circle the correct **bold** words in the sentences below.

There is only one horizontal force acting on the bus, pushing it to the left, so the forces on the bus are **balanced / unbalanced**.

Balanced / Unbalanced forces mean that the bus must change speed or direction. **Balanced / Unbalanced** forces mean that the bus cannot change speed or direction – if it was stationary, it will remain stationary.

Hint: Is it balanced or unbalanced forces which change motion? For help see P1 1.5 Balanced and unbalanced.

C Balanced forces mean that for each force acting on an object, there is an equal force acting in the opposite direction on the same object.

For each diagram below, circle whether the forces on the bus are balanced or unbalanced.

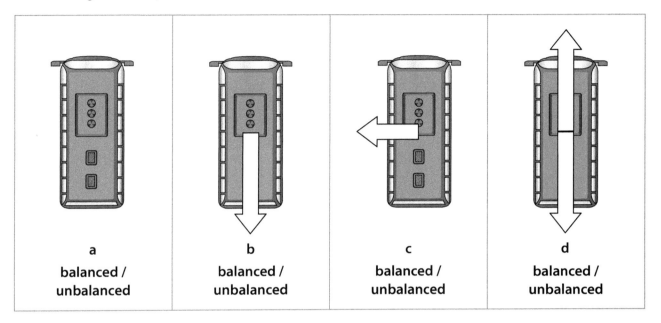

a	b	c	d
balanced / **unbalanced**	**balanced /** **unbalanced**	**balanced /** **unbalanced**	**balanced /** **unbalanced**

Hint: What does "balanced forces" mean? For help see P1 1.5 Balanced and unbalanced.

D Here is a diagram of a horizontal force acting on a bus.

Complete the sentences using some of these keywords:

road	equilibrium	interaction	right
bus	different	road	pairs	bus

Forces come in _____ called _____ pairs. Each force acts on a _____ object. The road pushes the bus to the left, as shown in the diagram. The _____ pushes the _____ to the _____. That is a force on the road, not the bus. The diagram shows forces on the _____ not the _____, so the diagram is correct.

Hint: How many objects are involved in an interaction pair? For help see P1 1.5 Balanced and unbalanced.

 Pinchpoint review
Now look back at the question – do you think you chose the right letter?
Turn to the Answers page to find out.

This is a repeat of activity D from P1 1.2 Squashing and stretching. Draw your graph here and then answer the questions on page 74.

D On the graph paper below, plot a graph of extension (*y*-axis) against force (*x*-axis) using the data in the table. Label the axes, and draw a line of best fit.

Force (N)	Extension (cm)
1.0	0.5
2.0	1.0
3.0	1.4
4.0	1.8
5.0	2.3
6.0	2.9
7.0	3.3
8.0	3.7

P2.1 Waves

A **a** Label the diagram using some of the key words from this list:

amplitude	wavelength	peak or crest	trough	frequency

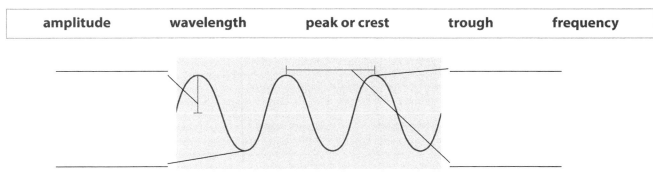

b Circle the correct **bold** word: this diagram shows a **transverse / longitudinal** wave.

B **a** Label the diagram using key words from this list:

wavelength	rarefactions	compressions

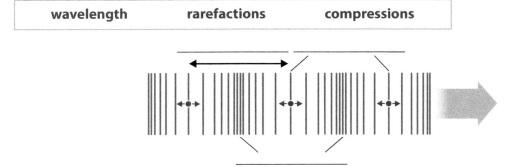

b Circle the correct **bold** word: this diagram shows a **transverse / longitudinal** wave.

C Draw a line to match each sentence's beginning with its correct ending.

Two waves that are out of step superpose	so it reflects to produce a reflected wave.
An incident wave hits a barrier	so they add up to produce a larger wave.
Two waves that are in step superpose	so they cancel out to produce a smaller wave.

What you need to remember

In science, a _____ is an oscillation or vibration that transfers _____ or information. _____ is the distance from the middle to the top of a wave. _____ is the number of waves that go past a particular point per second. _____ is the distance from one point on a wave to the same point on the next wave. The top of a wave is called a _____ or crest, and the bottom of a wave is called a _____. In a _____ wave, the oscillation is at 90° to the direction of the wave. In a _____ wave, the oscillation is parallel to the direction of the wave. When considering a slinky spring, in a compression the coils of the spring are _____. In a rarefaction the coils are _____. Waves bounce off surfaces and barriers. This is called _____. The wave coming into the barrier is called the _____ wave and the wave bouncing off the barrier is called the _____ wave. When waves are put together they _____ – they add up or cancel out.

P2.2 Sound and energy transfer

A In each sentence below, circle the object which is the **source** of the sound.

    a Someone speaks using their vocal cords.

    b A person is listening to music through the speakers of their headphones.

    c An elephant stamps its foot to warn other elephants of predators.

B Complete the sentences using some of the keywords given below.

vacuum	vibrate	medium	sound wave	speed of sound	particles

Something must _____ to produce a _____; it makes the air

molecules move backwards and forwards. Sound needs a _____ like a solid, liquid, or gas

to travel through. It cannot travel through empty space, a _____, because there are no

_____ to vibrate.

C Draw a line to match each observation with the most relevant explanation from each column.

We see fireworks before we hear them.	Light can travel through a vacuum.	The vibration is passed along more quickly than in a gas.

We can see the Sun, but not hear it.	The particles in a solid are very close together.	Light travels much faster than sound.

Sound travels fastest in solids.	Explosions give out light and sound at the same time.	Sound cannot travel through a vacuum; it needs a medium such as air to travel through.

D Draw a line to match each material with the speed of sound in that material.

steel	1500 m/s

air	5000 m/s

water	340 m/s

What you need to remember

An object must _____ to cause a sound wave. As it moves backwards and forwards, it causes

_____ in the medium to do the same. Sound needs a medium, whether solid, liquid, or gas, to travel

through. It cannot travel through a _____. Sound travels fastest in a _____ – this is

because the particles in a solid are closer together than in a liquid or a gas, so the vibration is passed along more

_____. _____ travels almost a million times faster than sound and does not need a

_____ to travel through.

P2.3 Loudness and pitch

A Circle the correct **bold** words in the sentences below.

You bang a drum **harder / softer** or bow a violin string with **less / more** force to produce a louder sound.

A loud sound has a bigger **amplitude / frequency** than a soft sound. It transfers **less / more** energy than a soft

sound. To make a louder sound, you need to make the vibration **bigger / smaller**.

B a Tick the wave below that shows a higher-pitched note.

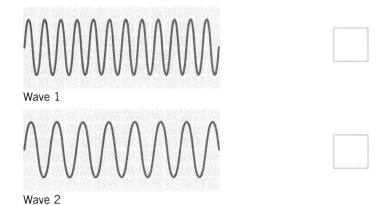

Wave 1

Wave 2

b Write a short sentence comparing the loudness of the two notes.

_____

c Give a reason for your answer. _____

C Here is a table showing the audible range for several species, including people.

Circle **true** or **false** to show whether or not a sound is heard by each species if there is a sound wave at 100 Hz or 40 000 Hz.

Species	Audible range (Hz)	Sound heard at 100 Hz?	Sound heard at 40 000 Hz?
Human	20–20 000	true / false	true / false
Bat	2000–110 000	true / false	true / false
Dog	67–45 000	true / false	true / false

What you need to remember

A loud sound has a bigger _____ than a quieter sound. A sound with high pitch has a higher

_____, which is measured in _____ (Hz). Humans cannot hear sound waves with a

frequency below _____ Hz; these are called _____. Humans cannot hear sound waves

with a frequency above 20 000 Hz; these are called _____. The range of frequencies that a human

or an animal can hear is called the _____ range. Many animals can hear frequencies that are much

_____ than the frequencies we can hear.

P2.4 Detecting sound

A Label the diagram of the ear using these keywords:

eardrum	cochlea	pinna
semi-circular canals		auditory nerve
auditory canal	ossicles	

B The statements below can be reordered to describe the process of you hearing someone speak. Read the statements and write down the order of statements you think will give the best description of this process.

Correct order ☐ ☐ ☐ ☐ ☐ ☐ ☐ ☐

1 pinna directs the sound wave

2 eardrum vibrates

3 sound wave travels through air

4 you hear the speech

5 vocal chords vibrate, creating a sound wave

6 ossicles amplify the sound

7 vibration reaches the cochlea

8 the signal travels down the auditory nerve

C We can compare the parts of a microphone to the parts of the ear.
Complete the sentences below with the name of the appropriate part of the ear.

When a singer sings into a microphone, the sound wave hits a flexible plate called a diaphragm. The diaphragm vibrates, like your _____. This produces an electrical signal, just like the cells in your _____. Wires carry an electrical signal, like your _____.

D Draw a line to correctly complete each sentence.

Listening to very loud music for a long time		can cause temporary damage until the hair cells have recovered.
A sharp object punching a hole in your eardrum		can cause permanent damage to your hair cells.
Listening to loud music for a short time		will cause temporary damage until the eardrum grows back.

What you need to remember

Your _____ detects sound waves by the outer ear or _____ collecting the waves and directing them along the _____ canal to the middle ear where the _____ vibrates. These vibrations pass to the _____, tiny bones that _____ the sound and pass the vibration through the oval window to the inner ear or _____. Here the liquid and _____ cells vibrate. Electrical signals are transmitted from here via the auditory _____ to the _____ and you hear the sound. Sound intensity is measured in _____ (dB). Exposure to very loud sounds can permanently _____ the hair cells in the cochlea so that you can become deaf.

A microphone has a flexible plate called a _____ that vibrates, producing an _____ signal. Loudspeakers vibrate, converting the electrical signal back to sound via an _____ to make the sound louder.

P2.5 Echoes and ultrasound

A Circle the correct **bold** words.

Ultrasound is made of **light / sound** waves that have a **frequency / amplitude** too **high / low** for people to hear, above **20 000 / 20** Hz.

B Some predators use echolocation to find their prey.
Draw a line to match each species with its reason for using echolocation.

Sperm whales hunt in deep water	when there is very little light to see by.
Some dolphins hunt across the seabed	so deep that there is too little light to see.
Bats hunt at night	to find prey buried out of sight.

C The statements below can be reordered to explain how doctors use ultrasound to make images of an unborn baby. Read the statements and write down the order of statements you think gives the best explanation.

Correct order ☐ ☐ ☐ ☐

1 a transmitter sends out a beam of ultrasound

2 a receiver detects the echo

3 the machine measures the time between the transmission and the echo and works out the distance travelled by the ultrasound to build up an image of the baby

4 the ultrasound wave travels through the woman and reflects off the baby, producing an echo

D Describe **two** ways (other than imaging unborn babies) that people use ultrasound.

_____

_____

What you need to remember

_____ is sound waves with a frequency too high for humans to hear, above _____ Hz.

It can be used for things like _____ , where a beam of ultrasound is sent out by a _____

under a ship. It travels through the water and _____ off the seabed. A _____ detects

the reflection and measures the _____ it took to transmit and receive the reflection from the seabed.

That allows us to work out how deep the sea must be. The reflection of a sound is called an _____ .

If lots of _____ join together to produce a longer sound, this is called a _____ .

Pinchpoint question

Answer the question below, then do the follow-up activity **with the same letter** as the answer you picked.

Here is a sound wave shown on the screen of an oscilloscope. The pitch of a sound relates to its frequency.

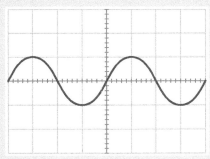

Which of the three sound waves, **X**, **Y**, and **Z** below, have a **higher pitch** than the sound wave above?

X

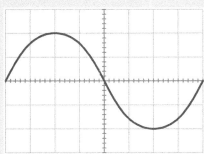

Y

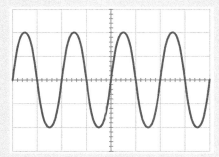

Z

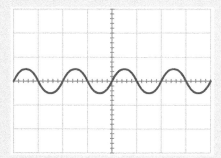

A   **X** and **Y**

B   **X** only

C   **Y** and **Z**

D   **Z** only

Follow-up activities

A The **loudness** of a sound relates to its amplitude: a **louder** sound has a wave that has a **larger** distance vertically from centre to peak and centre to trough.

The **pitch** of a sound relates to its frequency: a **higher**-pitched sound has a wave that has a **higher** frequency so there are more waves (shown by more peaks) in the same time interval.

Here is a sound wave shown on the screen of an oscilloscope:

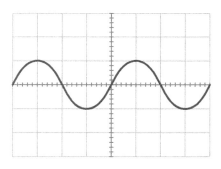

   a Compared to the sound wave on the right, which of the sound waves below, **Q** or **R**, is louder?

_____

Q

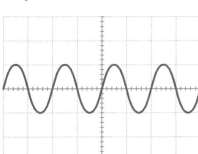

R

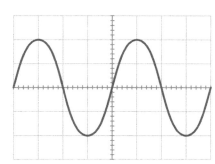

   b Which of the sound waves, **Q** or **R**, has a higher pitch? _____

Hint: Does pitch relate to amplitude or frequency? For help see P1 2.3 Loudness and pitch.

B The pitch of a sound relates to its frequency: a **higher** pitched sound has a wave that has a **higher** frequency.

In the two sound waves below, wave **S** has a higher frequency and therefore a higher pitch than wave **T**.

   S

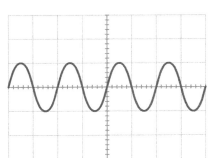

   T

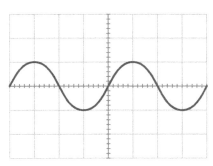

Describe **one** difference you can see in the waves **S** and **T** that shows you that sound wave **S** has a higher pitch than sound wave **T**.

Hint: Are the waves in a higher-pitched sound closer together or further apart? For help see P1 2.3 Loudness and pitch.

_____

_____

C Light has some similar properties to sound. The frequency of light relates to its colour, for example, violet light has a higher frequency than red light. The brightness of light relates to its amplitude, for example, bright violet light has a higher amplitude than dim violet light.

Wave **U** below represents a bright, red light. On the blank oscilloscope screen below, sketch a wave to represent a dim, violet light.

U

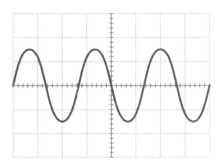 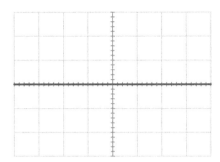

Hint: To which properties of a wave do brightness and colour relate? For help with this follow-up activity, see P1 3.5 Colour.

D a On the waves **V** and **W** below, label the amplitude and wavelength for each one.

V   **W**

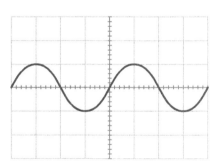 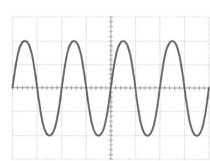

b Wave **W** has a higher frequency than wave **V**. How big is wave **W**'s wavelength compared to wave **V**?

_____

Hint: Does higher pitch mean higher or lower frequency? For help see P1 2.3 Loudness and pitch.

Pinchpoint review
Now look back at the question – do you think you chose the right letter?
Turn to the Answers page to find out.

P3.1 Light

A Complete the following sentences using **some** of the keywords given:

emits	transmits	absorbed	reflects	eye	source	scattered

You look at a book. A _____ of light, like a light bulb, _____ light. This light _____ off the book and into your eye. You see the book when the light is _____ in your _____.

B The statements below can be reordered to describe the process of seeing the Moon.
Read the statements and write down the order of statements that you think will give the best description.

Correct order: ☐ ☐ ☐ ☐ ☐

1 The moon is a non-luminous object.

2 Some of the reflected light is absorbed in your eye.

3 It does not emit light itself, it just reflects light from the Sun.

4 The Sun is a luminous object.

5 It is a source of light – it emits light waves through space.

C You are trying to look at three friends, but different materials are in the way of each friend. Draw a line to match each material to the description of what happens to the light from your friend and finally, what you can see.

transparent window glass		light is absorbed		you see your friend, but not clearly
opaque bricks of a wall		light is transmitted		you see your friend clearly
translucent frosted window glass		light is scattered		you cannot see your friend

D a How fast does light travel? _____ m/s

b It takes 500 seconds (8.3 minutes) to travel the 150 000 000 km from the Sun to the Earth. Astronomers say that the Earth is 8 light-minutes from the Sun.

How long will it take light from the Sun to reach Mars, which is 250 000 000 km from the Sun?

_____ seconds

Hint: Convert the speed of light from m/s to km/s to help you calculate your answer.

Remember that there are 1000 metres in a kilometre.

What you need to remember

_____ objects emit light: they are a _____ of light. Most objects are _____-_____ – they do not emit light. You can see objects when light is _____ off them and absorbed by your _____. Transparent substances _____ light. _____ substances do not. _____ substances transmit light, but it is _____. Light travels as a _____ through gases, some liquids like water, and some solids like glass. It can even travel through empty space, called a _____. The speed of light is about _____ m/s. Astronomers use '_____-_____' to measure distances in space.

P3.2 Reflection

A Circle the correct **bold** words in the sentences below.

When you look in the mirror, it appears that there is someone who looks just like you **in front of / behind** the mirror. The image is **upside down / upright** and **the same way round / laterally inverted** and appears **as far behind / twice as far behind** the mirror as you are in front. The image is a **virtual / real** image because you **could not / could** put a screen where the image appears and see an image on it. When you look at your mirror image in a flat, or plane, mirror, it is **a different / the same** shape and size.

B Complete the ray diagram below to show how an image of the candle is formed in a plane mirror.

mirror

object

C a Write down how the angle of reflection relates to the angle of incidence.

_____

b The diagram on the right shows one form of reflection.
Does it show specular reflection or diffuse scattering? _____

c Explain how the law of reflection causes this form of reflection.

_____

_____

_____

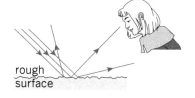

rough surface

What you need to remember

Light _____ off a mirror in the same way that a wave _____ off a barrier. The light that hits the mirror is called the _____ ray. The reflected light is called the _____ ray. An imaginary line at 90° to the mirror is called the _____. You measure angles from the normal to the rays of light. Rays reflect from surfaces with an angle of reflection _____ to the angle of _____. This is called the law of _____. With a flat or _____ mirror, the surface is smooth, causing _____ reflection; the reflected rays give a _____ image, as if there is someone the same shape and size as you the other side of the mirror. With a rough surface, there is _____ scattering, where no image is visible.

P3.3 Refraction

A Complete the ray diagram below to show what happens when light enters glass from air.

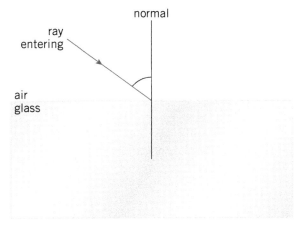

B Briefly explain the process of refraction shown in activity **A**. Try to use each of these keywords at least once:

refract	speed	slower	glass	air	direction

_____

_____

C This ray diagram shows light entering a rectangular block of glass.

   a Complete the ray diagram to show the ray emerging from the block.

   b Use these key words to label the diagram:

ray entering	refracted ray	normal
ray emerging	air	glass

D a Complete the ray diagram below, to show what happens when light travels through a lens.

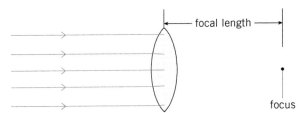

   b Complete the sentences below to describe what is happening in the diagram.

Light is _____ as it enters the curved surface of the lens and again as it leaves. It _____ to a

_____ .

What you need to remember

When light passes from one _____ into another it changes _____. This causes

it to change _____ ; a process called _____. If light goes from air into glass it

_____ and bends _____ the normal. This effect makes swimming

pools appear _____ than they are. The effect can be used to produce _____ or convex

lenses which bring light to a _____ or focal point.

A Label the diagram of the eye using these keywords:

optic nerve	**pupil**
cornea	**retina**
iris	**lens**

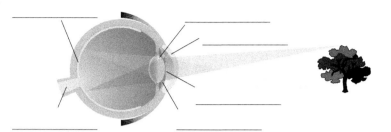

B Draw a line to match each part in the left-hand column with its function.

object	A hole that allows light to enter the lens.
cornea and lens	Controls the size of the pupil, allowing in more or less light.
iris	Real (you could put a screen here and you would see an image), inverted, smaller than the object.
pupil	Where the image forms – contains photoreceptors.
retina	Reflected light from this enters the eye.
photoreceptors	Rods and cones – absorb light causing a chemical reaction which produces an electrical signal.
image	Sends electrical signal to the brain.
optic nerve	Focus the light.

C Complete the sentences about the similarities between a pinhole camera and your eye. Use these key words:

retina	**pupil**	**image**	**pinhole**

Light enters the camera through the _____, just like it does through the _____ of your

eye. An _____ is formed on the screen, just like it is on your _____.

What you need to remember

Your eye works by _____ light reflected from an _____ you are looking at. Your cornea

and _____ focus the light. Your _____ controls the size of your _____,

letting through more or less light. A real (not virtual) inverted image is formed on your _____ where

_____ absorb the light, causing _____ reactions which send electrical signals along

the _____ nerve to your brain. Digital and pinhole cameras produce real images in a similar way. In a

digital camera, there is a grid of photosensitive _____ called a charge-coupled device (CCD). When

light hits each _____ they free _____ charges.

P3.5 Colour

A a Complete and label the ray diagram to show how and where a spectrum is formed. Label or show the colours of the spectrum in the order they appear.

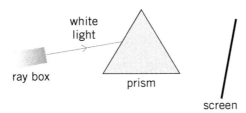

b Circle the correct **bold** words in the following sentences.

Dispersion happens with a prism because different colours of light are refracted by **the same amount / different amounts**. Violet light has a higher **frequency / amplitude** than red light. Violet is refracted the **least / most** and red the **least / most**.

B a Name the three primary colours that our eyes detect. _____

b Which secondary colour is made if we add red light to green light? _____

C Use the following key words to label the diagrams, to show the effect of filters on different colours of light:

no light	red light	blue light

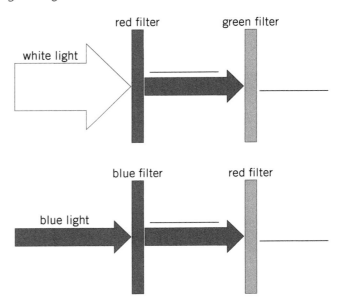

D Complete the table to show the colour that each object appears under red light.

Colour of object (as it appears in white light)	Colour that the object appears under red light
red	
green	
black	
white	

What you need to remember

Our eyes detect three _____ colours of light: red, green, and blue. Two of these colours of light

added together make _____ colours of light, for instance blue and green light added together make

_____ light. All three _____ colours of light added together make _____

light. Filters _____ light, for instance a blue filter _____ all colours except

_____ from white light.

Coloured objects subtract light by _____ only their own colour. For example, a blue object appears

blue because when white light falls on it, all colours are absorbed except _____, which reflects.

A _____ can be used to split up light into a _____ of different colours. It does this

because of _____: light with the highest _____ (violet) refracts more than light with the

_____ frequency (red). The spectrum from the Sun's light is _____ – it has no gaps.

Pinchpoint question

Answer the question below, then do the follow-up activity **with the same letter** as the answer you picked.

Which diagram and description below best describes how you see a friend in daylight?

A Light is emitted by the Sun. Some light travels to your friend where it illuminates her so you see her.

B Your friend emits light, which travels to your eye where it is absorbed so you see her.

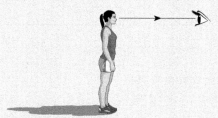

C You look at your friend. Light travels to your friend, where it is absorbed so that you see her.

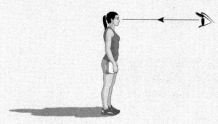

D The Sun emits light. Some reflects from your friend into your eye.

Follow-up activities

A Every surface reflects at least some light. On the diagram below, add the rays to show light being emitted by the lamp, reflecting off an old wooden table, and being absorbed in your eye so that you see the table.

Hint: Which direction must light be travelling when it hits your eye? For help see P1 3.1 Light.

B Every surface reflects at least some light, and another object, a light source, must have emitted that light elsewhere.

Use some of these keywords to complete the following sentences:

emits	absorbed	reflected	reflect	luminous	transmitted	non-luminous

A _____ object, such as the Sun, emits light. _____ objects, such as people, do not

emit light. However, they do _____ at least some light. We can see a non-luminous object when a

luminous object _____ light, which is _____ from the non-luminous object, and enters

our eye, where it is _____.

Hint: Revise the definitions for these words. For help see P1 3.1 Light.

C To see, light must reach your eye **from** the object you are looking at. In a diagram, this is shown with an arrow pointing from the object to your eye.

a What is the name for the cells in your retina where light is absorbed? _____

b Describe one thing that happens after light is absorbed in those cells.

_____

Hint: What other parts of the body are involved in vision? For help see P1 3.1 Light.

D One simple type of camera is shown below.

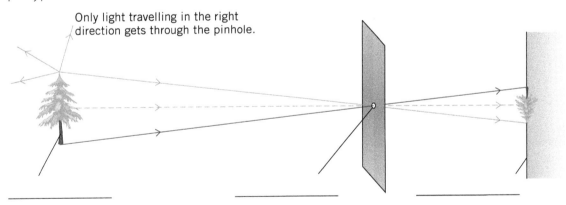

Only light travelling in the right direction gets through the pinhole.

_____   _____   _____

a Label the diagram.
Hint: What is the name for that type of camera? For help see P1 3.4 The eye and the camera.

b Name a piece of equipment that could be used to record the image. _____

 Pinchpoint review

Now look back at the question – do you think you chose the right letter?
Turn to the Answers page to find out.

P4.1 The night sky

A Name these **three** objects you can see in the night sky without a telescope.

a _____ b _____ c _____

B Re-order these space objects in order of their size, starting with the smallest.

Universe	galaxy	Solar System	planet	Sun	Moon

_____

C Draw a line to match each object with its description.

meteor	a natural, luminous object
Solar System	the Sun and everything that orbits it
galaxy	rock or dust that burns up as it passes through Earth's atmosphere
star	a collection of billions of stars

D Complete the table below about orbiting objects in our Solar System.

Object	What does it orbit?	Is it natural or artificial?
GPS satellite for satnav		
a moon		
a planet		
a comet		
International Space Station		

What you need to remember

We can see many different objects in the night sky without a telescope. The nearest are artificial _____ that _____ the Earth. The _____ is the Earth's only _____ satellite. We can also see five _____: Mercury, Venus, _____, Jupiter, and Saturn. Like Earth, they orbit the _____ and make up part of the _____ _____. We may also be lucky enough to see meteors or _____ in the night sky. The dots of light we see are _____ in our own _____, which is called the _____ _____. It is just one of billions of galaxies that make up the _____.

P4.2 The Solar System

A Circle which of these objects can be found in the Solar System.

galaxy	comet	meteor	asteroid	planet

B Draw a line to match each object with its description.

asteroid belt	made up of ice and dust; sometimes orbits close to the Sun, sometimes far
Sun	orbits Sun, may be rocky or gas giant
a planet	orbits a planet
a moon	made up of small rocky bodies, between Mars and Jupiter
a comet	in the centre of the Solar System

C Look at the data about the planets in the table.

Planet	Type	Diameter (km)	Distance from Sun (million km)
Mercury	rocky	4879	58
Venus	rocky	12 104	108
Earth	rocky	12 756	150
Mars	rocky	6787	228
Jupiter	gas giant	142 800	778
Saturn	gas giant	120 660	1427
Uranus	gas giant	51 118	2871
Neptune	gas giant	49 528	4498

a Give **one** similarity between the rocky planets and the gas giant planets.

_____

b Give **one** pattern in the diameters of the planets.

_____

c Give **one** pattern in the distances of the planets from the Sun.

_____

What you need to remember

At the centre of the _____ System is the _____. It is orbited by four inner

_____ and four outer _____. Each orbit is a squashed circle shape called an

_____. The inner planets are Mercury, _____, Earth, and _____. They

are all terrestrial planets; they are made of _____. The outer planets are Jupiter, Saturn, Uranus, and

Neptune. They are called _____ giants; they are made mainly of _____ and are very

cold and much bigger than the inner planets. Many planets have _____ that orbit them. Between

the inner and outer planets there is an _____ belt made up of thousands of pieces of rock. Pluto

used to be called a planet but is now called a _____ planet.

P4.3 The Earth

A Describe **one** physical difference between summer and winter.

_____

B Draw a line to match the object with the description and explanation of the apparent movement of the object in the sky.

| the Moon | | the Earth orbits the Sun once a year and the night-side of the Earth faces different constellations of stars during the year |

| the Sun | | the Earth spins on its axis once every 24 hours and so different regions of the Earth face the Sun at different times of day |

| stars | | orbits the Earth once a month |

C **a** Explain why London is an average of 14°C warmer in the middle of summer than the middle of winter.

_____

_____

_____

_____

_____

_____

b Describe and explain the difference in day length in London between summer and winter.

_____

_____

_____

_____

_____

What you need to remember

Once each _____, the Earth _____ on its axis, causing the Sun's apparent motion through the sky and giving us day and _____. Once each _____, the Earth _____ around the Sun. The differences between summer and winter in the UK are mainly caused by the _____ of the Earth's axis. In summer, the Northern Hemisphere tilts _____ the Sun, which means that each bit of the ground receives _____ of the Sun's rays; days are _____, and the Sun appears to rise _____ into the sky at noon.

P4.4 The Moon

A Explain why we can see the Moon from Earth.

_____

_____

B Look at the diagram of the Moon orbiting the Earth.

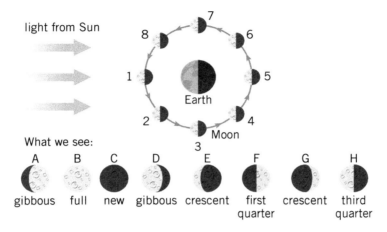

For each position 1–8 on the diagram, write down a letter A–H in the table below, to show which phase of the Moon is seen by someone on Earth.

Position	1	2	3	4	5	6	7	8
Phase of the Moon (A–H)								

C Explain briefly why total solar eclipses happen. Try to use all of the following key words:

Moon	**Sun**	**Earth**	**shadow**

_____

_____

_____

_____

What you need to remember

_____ of the Moon is lit by the _____ at all times. As it orbits the _____

we see different amounts of it illuminated by the Sun, causing the _____ of the Moon. When the side

facing the Earth is in shadow, we call it a _____ moon. Later, when we see the whole of the side lit by

the Sun, we call it a _____ moon. This cycle occurs once each lunar _____.

If the Moon is between the _____ and the _____, a shadow called the

_____ occurs on Earth, where the light from the Sun is totally blocked and there will be a total

_____ eclipse. The _____ occurs where only part of the Sun's light is blocked and a

partial _____ eclipse occurs. If the Earth comes between the Sun and the _____ and

blocks the Sun's light from reaching the Moon, a _____ eclipse can occur.

Pinchpoint question

Answer the question below, then do the follow-up activity **with the same letter** as the answer you picked.

Here are some observations about objects we see in the sky:

- The Sun appears to cross the sky once each day.

- Stars appear to cross the sky once each day.

- Different stars are visible in summer compared to winter.

Circle the correct explanation.

	Explanation
A	The Sun orbits the Earth once each day. The Earth spins on its axis once each year.
B	The Earth orbits the Sun once each day. The Earth spins on its axis once each day.
C	The Sun orbits the Earth once each day. Stars also orbit the Earth once each day.
D	The Earth spins on its axis once each day. The Earth orbits the Sun once each year.

Follow-up activities

A Images from artificial satellites orbiting the Earth show that the Earth spins on its axis once each day, not once each year.

Draw a labelled diagram showing the Earth both spinning on its axis and orbiting the Sun.
Label it to show which motion happens 'once per day' and which 'once per year'.

Hint: Day and night are due to the Earth spinning. For help see P1 4.3 The Earth.

B Complete the following sentences.

Day and night are caused by the Earth _____ on its axis, so the Earth takes _____ day to

spin once. A year is caused by the Earth _____ the Sun. A year is approximately _____

days, so the Earth spins _____ times for each complete _____ around the Sun.

Hint: How many days in one year? For help see P1 4.3 The Earth.

C Imagine that you are sitting on a bus that is driving forwards, looking ahead. Road signs appear to rush towards you, but it is of course you that is moving, not the road signs. In the same way, the apparent motion of the Sun or stars in the sky is caused by the Earth spinning and orbiting the Sun, not the other way around.

a The surface of the Earth spins from west to east. Which way would a stationary object in the sky appear to move?

_____

b This photograph of the night sky was taken over approximately 12 hours. It shows the path that stars appear to follow through the sky, but it is the Earth that is rotating on its axis.

In the time it takes the Earth to orbit the Sun, the Earth spins on its axis about 365 times. We call this period a year. Complete the sentences to explain why can we see different stars at night in the summer compared to in the winter, using some of the words below.

year   different   position   winter   axis   day

There is night and day on the Earth because it spins on its _____. The Earth moves around

the Sun once per _____. This means it is on opposite sides of the Sun in the summer and

_____ seasons. We see different stars at night in summer and winter because the Earth is in a

different _____ in its orbit around the Sun.

Hint: Does the Earth move? For help see P1 4.3 The Earth.

D A partial solar eclipse is caused when the Moon partially blocks out the light reaching the Earth from the Sun. On a separate piece of paper, sketch and label a diagram to illustrate how this happens, making sure you label the area on the Earth where a partial solar eclipse will be seen.

Hint: Where must the Moon be to cast a shadow? For help see P1 4.3 The Earth.

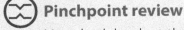 **Pinchpoint review**

Now look back at the question – do you think you chose the right letter?
Turn to the Answers page to find out.

P1 Revision questions

1　Circle an instrument that can be used to measure force.　**(1 mark)**

protractor　newtonmeter　mass balance

2　Circle which of the following are parts of the ear.
(3 marks)

pinna　　cochlea　　cornea
optic nerve　　ossicles　　pupil

3　A scientist passes light through a prism.

a　Circle the term that describes what happens to the light in the prism.　**(1 mark)**

addition　dispersion　focussing　emission

b　The light from the spectrum falls on to a white screen. What colours will appear on the screen in order starting with red?　**(1 mark)**

4　Explain why we can see the Moon. You may wish to use some of these key words. Not all are needed.　**(2 marks)**

Moon　Earth　Sun　emits　absorbs　reflects

5　The length of day (daylight hours) in Glasgow, UK changes through the year. Use **Figure 1** below to describe any patterns in the length of the day.　**(2 marks)**

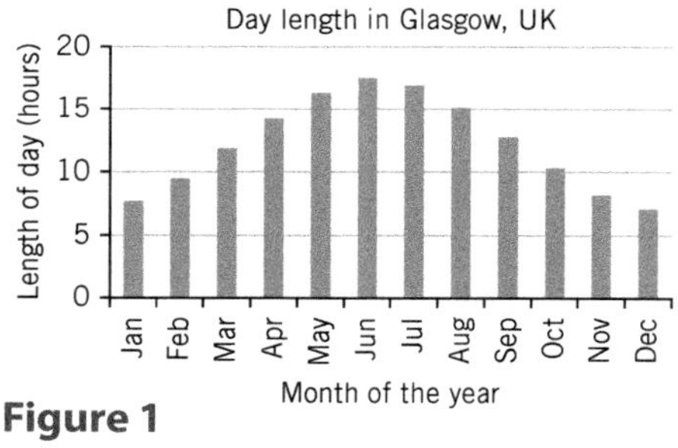

Figure 1

6　Two sound waves in the same place at the same time will **superpose**.
Define the term **superpose**.　**(2 marks)**

7　Various weights are hung from a spring.

a　Identify a force that acts at a distance in this situation.　**(1 mark)**

b　It is found that the spring obeys Hooke's Law. Give the relationship between force and extension.　**(1 mark)**

c　The spring stretches by 2 cm when a load of 5 N is applied. Predict the extension for a load of 10 N.　**(1 mark)**

＿＿＿＿＿＿＿＿＿ cm

8　Give **two** things that forces can change about objects.　**(2 marks)**

1＿＿＿＿＿＿＿＿＿＿＿＿＿＿＿

2＿＿＿＿＿＿＿＿＿＿＿＿＿＿＿

9　A cup is stationary on a table.

a　The forces on the cup are in equilibrium. Define the term **equilibrium**.　**(1 mark)**

b　Explain how the table provides a force that supports the cup.　**(3 marks)**

c　One interaction pair is the force of gravity on the cup due to the Earth, and the force of gravity on the Earth due to the cup. Describe why this is called an interaction pair.　**(2 marks)**

d　The cup has a mass of 0.2 kg. Use the following formula to calculate the weight of the cup, and give its units. g is 10 N/kg.

weight (N) = mass (kg) × gravitational field strength, g (N/kg)　**(3 marks)**

10 ⚗️⚗️ A skydiver jumps from a plane and speeds up initially. A while later she opens her parachute, slowing down. Discuss why she speeds up initially, and what causes the force when her parachute opens. (**6 marks**)

_____

_____

_____

_____

_____

_____

11 ⚗️⚗️ Waves can be either transverse or longitudinal. Describe the difference between transverse and longitudinal waves. (**2 marks**)

_____

_____

_____

_____

12 ⚗️⚗️ A group of scientists investigating whale behaviour used an underwater microphone to record the sounds emitted. They find that the speed of sound in seawater is 1500 m/s, compared to 340 m/s in air.

a Explain the difference in the speed of sound in water and air. (**2 marks**)

_____

_____

_____

_____

b Describe how the microphone detects the sounds emitted by the whales. (**3 marks**)

_____

_____

_____

13 ⚗️⚗️ A demolitions engineer has set explosives to bring down an old block of flats. She triggers the explosion.

a Explain whether she will hear the explosion first or see it first. (**2 marks**)

_____

_____

b Explain **two** potential consequences if she does not use sufficient hearing protection. (**2 marks**)

_____

_____

14 ⚗️⚗️ Penny sees a meteor one night and takes a photograph of it using her phone.

a Describe how her phone camera forms an image of the meteor. (**3 marks**)

_____

_____

_____

_____

b The light from the meteor takes time to travel to her phone. Circle the speed of light. (**1 mark**)

300 000 000 km/s   300 000 000 m/s

340 km/s   340 m/s

15 ⚗️⚗️ The lighting technician on a film set wants to produce different colours. He requires cyan but only has red, green, and blue lamps available.

a Describe how he can produce the secondary colour cyan from the primary colours. (**2 marks**)

_____

b The film set has some coloured glass that acts as a green filter. The technician tests the coloured glass to see whether light will emerge from it for each primary lamp, and if so, what colour light it is. Complete the table to show his findings. (**3 marks**)

Colour of lamp	Does light emerge from glass?	If yes, which colour?
red		
green		
blue		

16 🔺🔺 **Figure 2** shows the positions of the Moon and some of the stars in the constellations Capricorn and Sagittarius in the night sky.

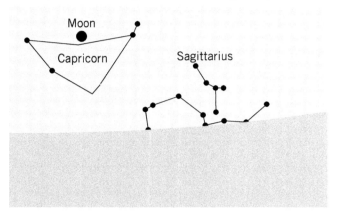

Figure 2 Day 1, 00:00

Figure 3 shows the same view of the night sky, one hour later.

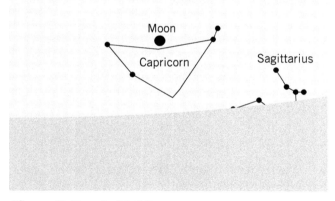

Figure 3 Day 1, 01:00

Figure 4 shows the same view of the night sky the next night at the same time as **Figure 2**.

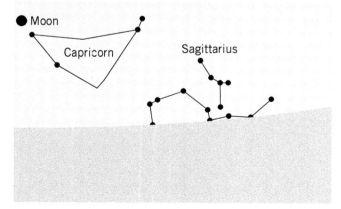

Figure 4 Day 2, 00:00

Explain how and why the positions of the Moon and stars are different in **Figures 3** and **4** compared to **Figure 2**.   **(4 marks)**

_____

_____

_____

_____

_____

_____

_____

_____

_____

17 🔺🔺 Describe **two** differences between the planets Mars and Neptune.   **(2 marks)**

_____

_____

_____

_____

P1 Checklist

Revision question number	Outcome	Topic reference	😞	😐	🙂
1	Know what instrument is used to measure forces. Know how to make measurements.	P1 1.1 WS1.3			
2	Name some parts of the ear.	P1 2.4			
3	State what happens to light when it passes through a prism.	P1 3.5			
4	Explain simply why we see the Moon from Earth.	P1 4.4			
5	Describe patterns in data linking day-length and month. Find a pattern in data.	P1 4.3 WS 1.4			
6	Describe what happens when waves superpose.	P1 2.1			
7a	Identify gravity as a force that acts at a distance.	P1 1.4			
7b	Describe Hooke's Law of proportional stretching.	P1 1.2			
7c	Use Hooke's Law to predict the extension of a spring.	P1 1.2			
8	Explain what forces do.	P1 1.1			
9a	Define equilibrium.	P1 1.5			
9b	Explain how solid surfaces provide a support force.	P1 1.2			
9c	Describe what is meant by an interaction pair.	P1 1.1			
9d	Describe the effect of gravitational forces on Earth and in space.	P1 1.4			
10	Explain why the speed or direction of motion of objects can change. Explain why drag forces and friction arise.	P1 1.5 P1 1.3			
11	Describe the different types of wave and their features.	P1 2.1			
12a	Explain why the speed of sound is different in different media.	P1 2.2			
12b	Describe how a microphone detects sound.	P1 2.4			
13a	Contrast the speed of sound and the speed of light.	P1 2.2			
13b	Explain some risks of loud music.	P1 2.4			
14a	Describe how a simple camera forms an image.	P1 3.4			
14b	State the speed of light.	P1 3.1			
15a	Describe how primary colours add to make secondary colours.	P1 3.5			
15b	Predict the colour of objects in red light and the colour of light through different filters.	P1 3.5			
16	Explain the motion of the stars and Moon across the sky.	P1 4.3			
17	Describe some similarities and differences between the planets of the Solar System.	P1 4.2			

Answers

WS1.1 and 1.2

A independent – the variable you change; dependent – the variable that changes because of the variable you change; control – a variable that must be kept the same during an investigation

B continuous – hair length, temperature, mass; discrete – number of ladybirds; categoric – eye colour, sex

C data, accurate, precise, repeatable, reproducible

What you need to remember

question, prediction, knowledge, independent, dependent, control, equipment, risk assessment, data, precise, reproducible

WS1.3

A

Angle (degrees)	Distance 1 (cm)	Distance 2 (cm)	Distance 3 (cm)	Mean distance (cm)

B 80 cm

C 51 cm

D x-axis, y-axis, unit, line graph, bar chart

What you need to remember

results, independent, measurements / readings / observations, mean, units, outliers, repeat, scale, x, line graph, bar chart, pie chart

WS1.4

A A line that goes through as many data points as possible, with equal numbers of points above and below the line.

B
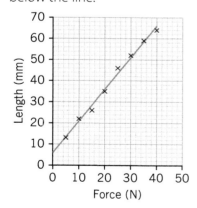

(Note: the y-intercept should be at length 6 mm, not pass through the (0, 0) origin.)

C As force increases, the length of the spring increases because the force causes the spring to unwind / extend. This matches the prediction.

What you need to remember

data, best fit, curve, conclusion, relationship, scientific, prediction

WS1.5

A discuss the quality of the data collected / suggest improvements to the method / specific examples, such as identifying outliers

B **two** from: used light-meters with different sensitivities / used lamps with different brightness / held light-meters at different angles / measured at different distances (or other reasonable suggestion)

C e.g., increase the range of distances / complete more repeat readings (or other reasonable improvement)

D a Group 2
   b more readings / smaller spread in data

E a e.g. digital mass balance measures to nearest 1 g; use a different balance which has smaller divisions (e.g. 0.01 g)
      temperature of the equipment suddenly drops because of a draught when someone opens a door; shield the equipment from draughts
   b e.g. spring balance reads 1 N even when there is no load – zero the spring balance before use; not looking straight on at a scale, so that all of the readings are too large – ensure you are level with a scale when you take a reading

What you need to remember

evaluate, quality, data, improvements, method, confidence, outliers, precise, more, random, systematic, range, more / repeat

Working Scientifically Pinchpoint

A this is an incorrect answer – these are **not** variables

B this is an incorrect answer – the dependent and independent variables are the wrong way round. The control variable is correct however

C this is the correct answer

D this is an incorrect answer – the control variable is incorrect – it is **not** a variable. The dependent and independent variables are correct however

Pinchpoint follow-up

A dependent variable – the variable that changes – time to dissolve
   independent variable – the variable that you change – water temperature
   control variable – the variables that must be kept the same – stirring speed

B

	dependent variable	independent variable(s)
a	height of sunflower	type of fertiliser
b	length of spring	number of masses
c	time taken for ice to melt	temperature
d	temperature change	different coloured materials
e	time for tea to cool	milk / no milk
f	volume of water	brand of nappy

C **a** size of beaker, stirring speed, person who times, mass of sugar cube, type of sugar
  b the higher the starting temperature of the water, the faster the sugar cube will dissolve
  c the higher the temperature, the faster the particles move and spread out
D all **except** water temperature (which in this case is the independent variable)

B1.1

A All living organisms are made up of cells. Cells are the smallest units found in an organism. Cells can only be seen through a microscope.
B slide – **Y**; eyepiece lens – **W**; objective lens – **X**; light – **Z**
C 5, 1, 2, 4, 3

What you need to remember
cells, microscope, magnifies, observation

B1.2

A

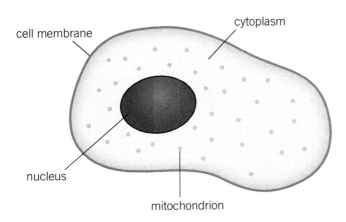

B nucleus – contains genetic material and controls the cell; mitochondria – where respiration occurs; chloroplast – where photosynthesis occurs; vacuole – contains cell sap to keep the cell firm; cell membrane – controls what comes in and out of a cell
C similarities – **two** from: both animal and plants cells contain a nucleus / mitochondria / cell membrane differences – **two** from: only plant cells have chloroplasts / a cell wall / a vacuole

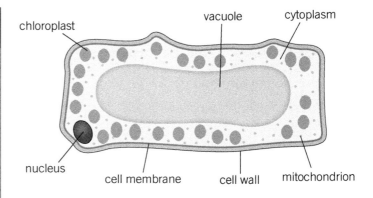

What you need to remember
nucleus, cytoplasm, cell membrane, mitochondria, cell wall, chloroplasts, vacuole

B1.3

A sperm cell – has a tail to swim; nerve cell – long and thin and transmits electrical impulses; root hair cell – has a large surface area to absorb water; leaf cell – contains lots of chloroplasts for photosynthesis
B 1 nerve cell; 2 sperm cell; 3 root hair cell; 4 leaf cell
C 1 true; 2 false; 3 true; 4 true; 5 false

What you need to remember
specialised, red blood, impulses, sperm, hair, water, chloroplasts

B1.4

A oxygen and glucose
B 2, 3
C S, **Q, P, R**
D high, root, low, vacuole, rigid, shrinks, floppy

What you need to remember
high, low, diffusion, oxygen, carbon dioxide

B1.5

A amoeba
B flagellum to help it to move; chloroplasts to make food by photosynthesis; eye spot to detect light

C animal cell

two reasons from: it has no chloroplasts / it has no cell wall / it has no large vacuole full of water.

What you need to remember

euglenas, unicellular, one, cytoplasm, chloroplasts, eye spot, flagellum

B1 Chapter 1 Pinchpoint

A this is the correct answer

B this is an incorrect answer – **not all** plant cells have chloroplasts

C this is an incorrect answer – plant and animal cells **do** have important differences

D this is an incorrect answer – **both** plant and animal cells have mitochondria

Pinchpoint follow-up

A it is not a plant cell as it does not contain a cell wall, vacuole or chloroplasts; it is specialised for its role in the reproductive system, and therefore an animal cell

B chloroplasts contain chlorophyll, which traps light needed for photosynthesis; root hair cells are found underground where no light is available so no need for chloroplasts

C

Cell component	✓ if found in plant cells	✓ if found in animal cells
nucleus	✓	✓
cell membrane	✓	✓
cell wall	✓	
cytoplasm	✓	✓
vacuole	✓	
chloroplast	✓	
mitochondria	✓	✓

D plant, respiration, energy, photosynthesis, respiration

B2.1

A tissue – group of similar cells working together; organ – group of different tissues working together; organ system – group of different organs working together

B cells ➔ tissues ➔ organs ➔ organ systems ➔ organism

C X – reproductive system – penis / uterus / vagina / ovaries / testes; Y – circulatory system – heart; Z – respiratory system – lungs

What you need to remember

multicellular, hierarchy, tissues, organ, organ system, organism

B2.2

A 1 trachea; 2 lungs; 3 rib; 4 diaphragm; 5 bronchi; 6 bronchiole; 7 alveoli

B Alveoli walls are only one cell thick. Alveoli create a large surface area.

C

Gas	Inhaled air	Exhaled air
carbon dioxide	less	more
nitrogen	same	same
oxygen	more	less

What you need to remember

respiratory, lungs, oxygen, exhale, trachea, bronchi / bronchus, alveoli / alveolus, gas exchange

B2.3

A rubber – diaphragm; balloon – lung; bell jar – chest cavity; tube – trachea

B contract, up and out, contracts, down, increases, decreases, into

C 6, 2, 4, 5, 3, 1

What you need to remember

ribs, contract, increases, decreases, relax, decreases, increases, out, bell jar, asthma, volume

B2.4

A 1 skull; 2 jaw bone; 3 collar bone; 4 vertebral column; 5 radius; 6 femur; 7 kneecap

B support – bones create a framework for muscles and organs to connect to; protection – stop vital organs from being damaged; movement – muscles pull on bones to make you move; making blood – tissue in centre of some bones makes blood cells

C skull – brain; vertebral column – spinal cord; ribcage – heart / lung

D bone marrow

What you need to remember

skeleton, protect, support, move, blood, marrow

B2.5

A found where two or more bones join together

B muscle contracts, muscle pulls on bone

C fixed – no movement – skull; ball and socket – all directions – shoulder; hinge – backwards and forwards – knee

D force, newton, greater, N

joints, movement, directions, ligaments, cartilage, contracts, force, newtons

B2.6

A 1 neck muscles; 2 biceps; 3 abdominal muscles; 4 calf muscles

B pair, joint, relaxes

C

Arm movement	Biceps	Triceps
bends	contracts	relaxes
straightens	relaxes	contracts

What you need to remember

tendons, shortens, bone, muscles, joint, antagonistic, relaxes

B1 Chapter 2 Pinchpoint

A this is an incorrect answer – the diaphragm moves **down**

B this is the correct answer

C this is an incorrect answer – air is **not** 'sucked' in, it is drawn in by changes to chest volume

D this is an incorrect answer – increasing chest volume **decreases** pressure in the lungs

Pinchpoint follow-up

A muscles between ribs contract and move up; the diaphragm contracts and moves down

B the airways of the person with asthma are inflamed (swollen) and produce lots of thick mucus; this narrows the airways and makes it harder for the person to breathe; therefore less oxygen reaches the lungs, and the person feels out of breath

C downwards, diaphragm, increases, decrease, in

D **a** when the molecules hit the wall, they apply a (pushing) force onto the walls of the container

   b less, decreases, in

B3.1

A adolescence, sex hormones, puberty, 9–14

B boys: voice deepens, shoulders widen, testes start to produce sperm
girls: breasts develop, periods start, hips widen, ovaries start to release egg cells

C **two** from: pubic hair / underarm hair / grow taller / body odour

What you need to remember

adolescence, physical, puberty, sex hormones, taller, pubic / underarm, break / deepen, shoulders, periods, hips

B3.2

A 1 cervix; 2 ovary; 3 oviduct; 4 uterus; 5 vagina

B 1 testis; 2 sperm duct; 3 glands; 4 urethra; 5 penis; 6 scrotum

C ovaries – contain eggs; uterus – where a baby develops until it is born; oviducts – carry egg to uterus; vagina – receives sperm during sexual intercourse

D penis – places sperm in vagina; glands – produce nutrients to keep sperm alive; sperm ducts – carry sperm from testes to penis; testes – produce sperm

What you need to remember

sperm, vagina, testes, sperm ducts, penis, egg, oviducts, uterus

B3.3

A egg, month, an ovary, cilia, uterus

B 1 true; 2 false; 3 true; 4 true; 5 false

C fertilisation – the nuclei of the sperm and egg cell join together; ejaculation – semen containing sperm is released into the vagina; implantation – the embryo attaches to the lining of the uterus

D oviduct

What you need to remember

gametes, sperm, egg, ovary, cilia, ejaculation, nucleus / nuclei, fertilisation, embryo, uterus, implantation

B3.4

A gestation, 9, blood

B 1 placenta; 2 umbilical cord; 3 uterus; 4 fetus; 5 fluid sac; 6 cervix

C placenta – organ where substances pass between mother's and fetus's blood; umbilical cord – connects the fetus to the placenta; fluid sac – acts as a shock absorber protecting the fetus from any bumps; cervix – keeps the fetus in the uterus until it is ready to be born

D relaxes, uterus, vagina

What you need to remember

uterus, gestation, 9, sac, oxygen, blood, placenta, umbilical cord, cervix, uterus, vagina

B3.5

A 4, 3, 1, 2

B uterus, fertilised, menstrual, period, ovulation

C day 14

D uterus lining will remain thick, periods will stop

E **two** from: condom, contraceptive pill, diaphragm, IUD, other appropriate suggestion

What you need to remember

menstrual, egg, ovulation, lining, period

B3.6

A 1 filament; 2 anther; 3 petal; 4 stigma; 5 style; 6 ovary; 7 sepal

B anther – produces pollen; stigma – sticky to 'catch' pollen; ovary – contains ovules

C Transfer of pollen from the anther to the stigma.

D wind-pollinated: large quantities of pollen, pollen with low mass, brown or dull green flowers, anther and stigma hang outside the flower
insect-pollinated: brightly coloured flowers, nectar, sweet-smelling flowers, anther and stigma inside the flower

What you need to remember

pollen, anther, insects, brightly, nectar, sweet, large, light / low mass, stigma

B3.7

A **a** 1 ovule; 2 ovule nucleus; 3 pollen grain; 4 pollen nucleus
b Drawing to show pollen tube growing down to ovule. Label describes pollen nucleus travelling down the pollen tube to join with the ovule nucleus.

B stigma, pollen tube, style, ovule, fertilisation, fruit, seeds

C water, oxygen, warmth

What you need to remember

fertilisation, pollen, ovule, fruit, seeds, germinate, warmth

B3.8

A The movement of seeds away from the parent plant.

B wind – small mass and extensions that act as parachutes or wings; animal (internally) – seeds contained in bright, sweet fruits; animal (externally) – hooks to attach to fur; water – small mass allowing them to float; explosive – fruits burst open when they are ripe, throwing seeds in different directions

C **a** wind **b** explosive / explosion

D independent variable – length of seed wing; dependent variable – distance the seed travels; control variable – height seed is dropped from

What you need to remember

dispersed, competition, space, wind, animals

B1 Chapter 3 Pinchpoint

A this is the correct answer

B this is incorrect – the fetus does **not** breathe. Other substances are also transferred.

C this is incorrect – blood itself is **not** transferred.

D this is incorrect – the placenta transfers substances between the mother's and the fetus's blood.

Pinchpoint follow-up

A large surface area due to presence of villi; rich blood supply to transport substances to / from fetus to maintain concentration gradient; only a few cells thick to minimise diffusion distance

B oxygen, carbon dioxide, born, fluid, respire, glucose, oxygen, placenta, diffuse

C 1 false; 2 true; 3 false; 4 false; 5 false; 6 true

D mother to fetus: oxygen, glucose, antibodies
fetus to mother: carbon dioxide, urea

B1 Revision questions

1 **a** female – ovary, oviduct, uterus [1]; male – penis, sperm duct, testis [1]
b **i** breasts develop / hips widen / periods start / eggs released [1]
ii voice breaks / sperm produced / testes or penis get bigger / hair growth on face or chest [1]
iii pubic hair / underarm hair / growth spurt / body odour [1]

2 **a** **A** cell membrane [1]; **B** cytoplasm [1]; **C** mitochondrion [1]; **D** nucleus [1]
b **two** from: vacuole [1]; cell wall [1]; chloroplasts [1]
c microscope [1]

3 **a** cell → tissue → organ → organ system → organism [no mark for organism; 1 mark for each correct sequential structure, e.g. organ following tissue]
b **i** stomach / pancreas [1]
ii lung [1]
iii leaf [1]

4 **a** sperm cell – tail; leaf cell – lots of chloroplasts; egg cell – fat store [2 marks for 3 correct, 1 mark for 2 correct]
b **i** e.g., nerve cell / red blood cell / egg cell [1]
ii e.g., root hair cell [1]

5 **a** **X** petal [1]; **Y** stigma [1]; **Z** filament [1]
   b **i** reproductive / sex cell [1]
      ii anther [1]
      iii ovary [1]
   c insect-pollinated, e.g. tulip / daisy / sunflower [1]; wind-pollinated, e.g. grass / corn / wheat [1]
   d the nuclei of the pollen and ovule / male and female plant gametes [1] join together / fuse [1]

6 **a** nucleus – controls the activities of the cell [1]; vacuole – stores sap and helps to keep the cell firm [1]; cytoplasm – where the cell's chemical reactions take place [1]
   b [Contain chlorophyll] to enable the plant to photosynthesise [1]

7 **a** **six** from: take thin slice of onion material [1]; place on slide [1]; add cover slip [1]; add stain to help view some structures [1]; move microscope stage to its lowest position [1]; place the slide on the stage [1]; select (the objective lens with) the lowest magnification [1]; look through the eyepiece [1]; adjust the coarse focus knob until the cells come into view [1]; then adjust the fine focus knob until the cells are in focus [1]; increase the magnification (use an objective lens with a higher magnification) to view structures more clearly / in more detail [1]
   b sketch shows: a number of cells in a regular pattern [1]; a minimum of three correctly labelled components [3]
   c **i** cellulose [1]
      ii (the cellulose is strong, so the) cell wall is rigid [1] to provide support for the cell / plant [1]

8 **a** alveoli / alveolus [1]
   b transfers gas between lungs and blood [1]; CO_2 out **and** O_2 in [1]
   c large surface area [1] and thin wall / wall only one cell thick [1] to maximise rate of diffusion [1]

9 **a** volume = difference between water levels / 4.0 – 0.5 [1] = 3.5 litres [1] [accept correct value for 2 marks without working]
   b **two** from: exhaled air has: lower proportion of oxygen [1]; higher proportion of carbon dioxide [1]; higher proportion of water vapour [1]; is warmer [1] (or converse)
   c e.g., asthma / smoking [1]

10 **a** mean = $\frac{450 + 410 + 370}{3}$ [1]
       = 410 [1] N [1]
   b e.g., muscle fatigue [1]
   c **three** from: the two muscles are antagonistic [1]; as the biceps contracts, the triceps relaxes [1],

moving the lower arm upwards [1]; as the triceps muscle contracts, the biceps muscle relaxes [1], moving the lower arm upwards [1]

11 **a** B [1] and C [1]
   b percentage = $\frac{8}{20} \times 100$ [1]
       = 40% [1]
   c **two** from: an animal will be attracted to eat the plant [1]; the sticky coating on the seeds will stick to the animal's body / fur [1]; the seeds will then be deposited in another area [1]

12 **a** cervix [1]
   b shock absorber / protects against bumps [1]
   c **four** from: substances pass between mother's and fetus's blood [1]; oxygen passes to fetus [1]; nutrients pass to fetus [1]; carbon dioxide passes to mother [1]; placenta prevents harmful substances reaching fetus [1]; prevents infections reaching fetus [1]

C1.1

A materials – the different types of stuff that everything is made from; substances – made of just one type of material, every particle is the same; properties – what a material looks like and how it behaves; particles – the tiny things that everything is made from
B the same size as, the same, greater, greater
C Y is liquid water and Z is ice

What you need to remember

particles, different, looks, behaves, arranged, move

C1.2

A 1, 3
B solid – **a**; liquid – **c**; gas – **b**
C A solid does not flow because its particles do not move around. A gas has no fixed shape because its particles move around. You cannot easily compress a liquid because its particles touch each other.

What you need to remember

gas(eous), matter, movement, different

C1.3

A melting – the change of state from solid to liquid; freezing – the change of state from liquid to solid
B sodium, titanium
C left – 1 and 5; middle – 3 and 4; right – 2 and 6

What you need to remember

melting, faster, away, melting, pure, freezing, slowly

C1.4

A 1, 3, 5, 4, 2

B When water boils bubbles of steam form everywhere in the liquid. Boiling water has water in both the liquid and gas states. In boiling water, the particles in the liquid touch other particles. In boiling water, the particles in the bubbles of steam are spread out. In boiling water, steam bubbles rise to the surface of the liquid and escape to the air.

C from top – liquid, gas, solid, solid

What you need to remember

gas, gas, liquid, conserved, boiling

C1.5

A liquid to gas – evaporation or boiling; solid to gas – sublimation; gas to liquid – condensation

B surface, everywhere in, slowly, closer together, condensation

C place (where the Petri dish is) – independent variable; amount of water – control variable; time for all the water to evaporate – dependent variable

What you need to remember

gas, surface, condensation, sublimation

C1.6

A examples of diffusion – the smell of perfume reaching your nose from someone's neck; a drop of ink spreading through water without stirring

B independent, dependent, control

C diagram showing particles spread out randomly all around the room

What you need to remember

mixing, gas, diffusion, stir

C1.7

A whole, in all directions, all the, the walls, area

B 1, 4

C The greater the number of gas particles in a container, the higher the pressure.
If you remove some gas particles from a container, the pressure decreases.
The higher the temperature of a gas in a container, the higher the pressure.
If you heat up a gas in its container, the pressure increases.

What you need to remember

all, collide, force, pressure

C1 Chapter 1 Pinchpoint

A this is an incorrect answer – the particles do **not** change size

B this is the correct answer

C this is an incorrect answer – the particles in liquid water are touching, so they **cannot** get closer together

D this is an incorrect answer – the volume of water stays the same, and the particles in liquid water do move around all the time; however, the movement of the particles **does not explain** why the volume stays the same

Pinchpoint follow-up

A three, the same size, identical, never, different, differently, differently

B the plunger has been pressed in; the same number of particles are present, but they are closer together

C **a** **i** the particles are randomly arranged; the particles are at the bottom of the container;
    ii the particles are not touching each other
  b particles are randomly arranged, are at the bottom of the box, **and** are touching each other

D a liquid flows – its particles move around, sliding over each other; a liquid cannot be compressed – its particles cannot get closer together; a gas can be compressed – its particles can get closer together; a gas has no fixed shape – its particles move around in the whole container; a solid does not change shape unless it melts or breaks – its particles are in fixed positions

C2.1

A 2, 3

B hydrogen – H; carbon – C, helium – He, calcium – Ca; zinc – Zn, tungsten – W; iron – Fe

C three, cannot, Au, Ag, Cu

What you need to remember

cannot, Periodic, chemical, symbols

C2.2

A elements – W and Y; not elements – X and Z

B An atom is the smallest part of an element that can exist. The atoms of copper are all the same as each other. A single atom of the element copper does not have the properties of a piece of copper.

C smallest, mercury, mercury, many

What you need to remember

atoms, smallest, atoms, different, many

C2.3

A from top: compound, element, atom, molecule

B an element, an element, two, a compound, different from, joined

C **a** elements – top left and bottom right
   b compounds – top right and bottom left

What you need to remember

two, strongly, different, one, molecule

C2.4

A (from top) 1, 2, 1, 2, 3, 2

B magnesium oxide – MgO – magnesium and oxygen
sodium chloride – NaCl – sodium and chlorine
carbon dioxide – CO_2 – carbon and oxygen
sulfur dichloride – SCl_2 – sulfur and chlorine
calcium sulfate – $CaSO_4$ – calcium, sulfur, and oxygen

C (left, from top) H_2, H_2O; (right from top) CO_2 and CH_4

What you need to remember

chemical, number, oxygen, one

C1 Chapter 2 Pinchpoint

A this is an incorrect answer – the properties of a compound are **different** from the properties of the elements that are in it

B this is an incorrect answer – the properties of a compound are **different** from the properties of the elements that are in it

C this is the correct answer

D this is an incorrect answer – the atoms of the different elements in a compound are strongly joined together, **not** just mixed up

Pinchpoint follow-up

A different from, solid, gas, magnesium oxide, does not

B 2, 3, 5

C (from top) element, compound, compound, compound, element compound

D A compound is a substance that is made up of atoms of two or more elements. The atoms of the different elements in a compound are strongly joined together. In sulfur dioxide, atoms of sulfur and oxygen are strongly joined together. Sulfur dioxide is made up of atoms of two elements.

C3.1

A (from top) sees, smells / sees, feels, hears

B useful – making a medicine, a tree making wood; not useful – a car going rusty, breakfast cereal going stale

C 1, 4

D Melting is an example of a physical change. It is easy to get back the starting substances in a physical change. New substances are made in a chemical change. Dissolving is an example of a physical change.

What you need to remember

new, rearranged, differently, not, energy, catalysts, physical

C3.2

A reactants, reactant, product, elements, compound

B **a** reactants – iron and sulfur; product – iron sulfide
   b reactants – methane and oxygen; products – carbon dioxide and water
   c reactant – copper carbonate; products – copper oxide and carbon dioxide

C **a** sodium + chlorine ⟶ sodium chloride
   b aluminium + iodine ⟶ aluminium iodide
   c propane + oxygen ⟶ carbon dioxide + water

D (top line) oxygen molecule
(bottom line, from left) reactant molecules, product molecules

What you need to remember

reactants, products, left, right, arrow

C3.3

A fuel – a material that burns to transfer energy by heating; combustion – the scientific word for burning; oxidation – any reaction in which a substance reacts with oxygen; rusting – an oxidation reaction that is not useful

B (from top) carbon dioxide; water; carbon dioxide and water

C independent variable – fuel; dependent variable – increase in temperature of water; control variables – volume of water, distance of flame from test tube

What you need to remember

energy, combustion, oxygen, carbon dioxide, water, oxygen

C3.4

A 1, 2, 4

B copper carbonate decomposed most quickly; lead carbonate decomposed more slowly than copper carbonate; potassium carbonate did not decompose

C W and Z

What you need to remember

one, two, compound, compounds, oxide, carbon dioxide, thermal

C3.5

A equal to, melting, does not change, conservation

B 3, 1, 2, 4

C magnesium, magnesium oxide, increased, gas, the same as, 0.08 g

What you need to remember

physical, products, conservation, reactants

C3.6

A A chemical reaction involves energy transfers. An exothermic reaction transfers energy from the reaction mixture to the surroundings. An endothermic reaction transfers energy from the surroundings to the reaction mixture.

B (top row) 8; (bottom row) 25

C increase, exothermic, more, more

What you need to remember

energy, exothermic, transferred, endothermic, surroundings

C1 Chapter 3 Pinchpoint

A this is the correct answer

B this is an incorrect answer – the reactants are the starting substances in a reaction. They are on the left of the arrow. In this reaction, the reactants are methane and oxygen.

C this is an incorrect answer – the reactants are the starting substances in the reaction. They are on the left of the arrow. In this reaction, the reactants are methane and oxygen.

D this is an incorrect answer – methane and oxygen are not the same as carbon dioxide and water, although all together they do have the same number of each type of atom. The arrow means 'reacts to make'.

Pinchpoint follow-up

A **a** hydrogen + oxygen ⟶ water

    b iron + chlorine ⟶ iron chloride

    c butane + oxygen ⟶ carbon dioxide + water

    d copper carbonate ⟶
                         copper oxide + carbon dioxide

B **a** reactants – sulfur and oxygen, product – sulfur dioxide

    b reactants – aluminium and chlorine, product – aluminium chloride

    c reactants – ethane and oxygen, products – carbon dioxide and water

    d reactant – zinc carbonate, products – zinc oxide and carbon dioxide

C The reactants are shown on the left of the arrow. The products are shown on the right of the arrow. The products are carbon dioxide and water. The arrow means reacts to make. The equation shows that ethane and oxygen react together to make carbon dioxide and water.

D 2, 3

C4.1

A Lemon juice is an acid. Toothpaste is an alkali. If something feels soapy it is likely to be an alkali. If something tastes sour it is likely to be an acid.

B

Risk from this hazard	How to control this risk
burning your skin	wear gloves
damaging your eyes	wear safety glasses

C Y, X, X, water

What you need to remember

sour, soapy, corrosive, skin, dilute

C4.2

A acid – red or orange or yellow; alkali – blue or purple; neutral – green

B 4, 3, 1, 5, 2, 6

C (from top) acidic, neutral, alkaline

D pH 1–6 – gradual change from red to orange to yellow; pH 7 – green; pH 8–14 – gradual change from blue–green to blue to purple.

What you need to remember

neutral, red, neutral, alkaline, pH, less / lower, neutral, more / greater

C4.3

A base – a substance that neutralises an acid; alkali – a soluble base; neutralisation – when an acid reacts with a substance that cancels it out

B adding a base to a lake with acidic water; adding an acid to soil of pH 9

C (from top) dependent, control, independent, control, control

D beaker, indicator, 2, spatula, stirring rod, 5, increased, neutralised

What you need to remember

neutralised, increases, decreases

C4.4

A 1, 2

B hydrochloric acid – chlorides; sulfuric acid – sulfates; nitric acid – nitrates

C **a** reactants – magnesium and hydrochloric acid; salt – magnesium chloride

 b reactants – zinc oxide and sulfuric acid; salt – zinc sulfate

 c reactants – copper oxide and hydrochloric acid; salt – copper chloride

D **a** magnesium + hydrochloric acid ⟶
 magnesium chloride + hydrogen

 b zinc oxide + sulfuric acid ⟶ zinc sulfate + water

 c copper oxide + hydrochloric acid ⟶
 copper chloride + water

E **a** (left) salt solution; (right, from top) evaporating basin, beaker, boiling water

 b compound, acid, metal, compound

What you need to remember

salt, chloride, sulfate, hydrogen

C1 Chapter 4 Pinchpoint

A this is an incorrect answer – solution Z is neutral; it is **less** acidic than solutions X and Y. The lower the pH, the more acidic the solution.

B this is an incorrect answer – solution Z is **not** alkaline, it is neutral

C this is an incorrect answer – as acidity increases, pH decreases. This means that solution X is **more** acidic than solution Y.

D this is the correct answer

Pinchpoint follow-up

A L, K, M, J, N

B acidic, more, alkaline, higher

C (from left) Y, V, X, W, Z

D 2, 5, 6

C1 Revision questions

1 the substance is a liquid – bottom diagram [1]; the particles are vibrating on the spot – middle diagram [1]; you cannot pour the substance – middle diagram [1]; the substance condenses to make a liquid – top diagram [1]

2 **a** A [1]   **b** C [1]   **c** B [1]

3 reactants [1]

4 New substances are made. [1] Atoms are rearranged and join together differently. [1]

5 atom – the smallest particle of an element that can exist [1]; base – a substance that neutralises an acid [1]; compound – a substance made up of atoms of two or more elements, strongly joined together [1]; fuel – a substance that burns to transfer energy by heating [1]

6 1 – a very acidic solution [1]; 6 – a slightly acidic solution [1]; 7 – a neutral solution [1]; 14 – a very alkaline solution [1]

7 **six** from: in a solid the particles vibrate on the spot [1] but in a liquid the particles move around [1], sliding over each other [1]; in a solid the particles are arranged in a regular pattern [1] but in a liquid the particles are arranged randomly [1]; this means a liquid can flow [1] and takes the shape of its container [1], but a solid cannot flow [1] and has a fixed shape [1]; in both a solid and a liquid the particles are touching their neighbours [1]; this is why you cannot compress either a solid or a liquid [1]

8 **a** all points plotted correctly [2; between 5 and 9 points plotted correctly – 1]

 b 70 [1]

 c liquid [1]

 d solid [1]

9 **a** Al [1]

 b a substance that is made of one type of atom [1] that cannot be broken down into new substances [1]

 c the appearance of a compound is different from the appearance of the elements it is made from [1]

 d flame observed [1]; properties / appearance of product different from properties / appearance of reactants [1]

10 (from top) N_2 [1], NO [1], NO_2 [1], O_3 [1]

11 **a** 2 [1]

 b $(2 \times 10) = 20$ [1]

12 X is an element [1] but Y is a compound [1]; a molecule of X is made up of two atoms [1] but a molecule of Y is made up of three atoms [1]

13 **a** copper oxide [1]

 b copper chloride [1] and water [1]

 c stir **or** heat [1]

 d copper oxide [1]

 e heat over a water bath **or** stop heating when about half the water has evaporated and leave in a warm place for a few days [1]

 f wear eye protection [1]; do not touch hot apparatus [1]

14 **a** X [1]   **b** W [1]   **c** Y [1] and Z [1]

 d W [1]   **e** W [1]

15 a the mixture glows bright red [1]

b mass of reactants = mass of products

mass of bromine + mass of iron =

mass of iron bromide

mass of bromine = mass of iron bromide –

mass of iron

= 5.3 g – 1 g [1]

= 4.3 g [1]

16 a X [1]

b Y [1]

c they are both the same size [1]

d the atoms of Z have a greater mass than the atoms of Y, and they are the same size [1] so a piece of Z has a greater mass than a piece of Y of the same size [1]

e X [1] because atoms of X have a greater mass than atoms of Z [1] and the atoms of the two elements are the same size [1]

P1.1

A force of gravity

B 1.5 N

C A force of friction of the road on the tyre makes a bus change speed. A force of air resistance of the air on their parachute helps a skydiver land safely. A force of gravity of the Earth on the water makes spilt water spread into a puddle.

D gravity, person, Earth

What you need to remember

push, pull, move, direction, shape, gravity, friction / air resistance, air resistance / friction, interaction, measured, newtons / N

P1.2

A deforms, compress, stretch

B 2, 1, 4, 3

C 10 cm

D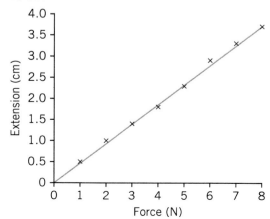

yes; the graph is a straight line / force has a linear relationship to extension (or other way round) / force is proportional to extension.

What you need to remember

deform, compress, pushes, reaction, stretch, extension, tension, double, Hooke's Law, proportional, elastic

P1.3

A water resistance – must push many liquid particles out of the way – a dolphin swimming

air resistance – must push many gas particles out of the way – a bird flying

friction – rough surfaces are touching – brakes on a bus

B A boat when its engine stops – water resistance causes boat to slow

A mechanic putting oil on a bicycle chain – to reduce friction between metal parts

Walking forwards on a pavement – without friction your shoe would slip uselessly on the pavement, like on ice

A skydiver opening her parachute – air resistance causes the skydiver to fall more slowly

C

Mistake	Correction
pulley	newtonmeter
should not change both surface and speed at the same time	keep either surface or speed the same

What you need to remember

friction, rough, lubrication, air, water (either order), streamlined, slow down

P1.4

A acts at a distance – magnetic, gravitational; contact force – water resistance, friction, air resistance

B newton, weight, kilogram, mass

C a force, masses, gets weaker

D 200

E Earth's surface – 1600; orbit – 1400; Moon's surface – 260 (to 2 s.f.); far from any star or planet – 0

What you need to remember

fields, non-contact, charge, charge, stronger, gravitational, decreases, gravity, mass

P1.5

A balanced, gravity, equal to, support force, horizontal

B **a** the forward force is greater than the backward force

b unbalanced

c no

C

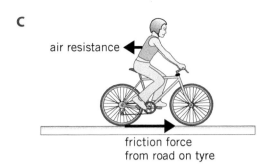

air resistance

friction force
from road on tyre

D likely to be moving with constant speed or stationary

What you need to remember

balanced, equilibrium, direction, speed, unbalanced, direction, speed (either order), driving, resistive

P1 Chapter 1 Pinchpoint

A this is the correct answer

B this is an incorrect answer; the bus **cannot** remain stationary because it has an unbalanced force acting on it, so it is accelerating

C this is an incorrect answer; there is a force pushing to the left with **no** balancing force pushing to the right

D this is an incorrect answer: forces **do** always act in pairs; however, the second one of the pair acts on a different object (the bus pushes the **road** to the right) so should not be shown on this diagram

Pinchpoint follow-up

A

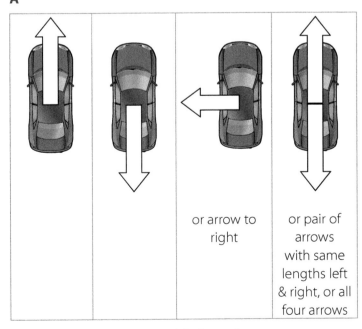

| | | or arrow to right | or pair of arrows with same lengths left & right, or all four arrows |

B unbalanced, unbalanced, balanced

C **a** balanced **b** unbalanced
c unbalanced **d** balanced

D pairs, interaction, different, bus, road, right, bus, road

P2.1

A **a** (clockwise from top-left) amplitude, peak or crest, wavelength, trough
b transverse

B **a** (clockwise from top-left) wavelength, rarefactions, compressions
b longitudinal

C Two waves that are out of step superpose so they cancel out to produce a smaller wave. An incident wave hits a barrier so it reflects to produce a reflected wave. Two waves that are in step superpose so they add up to produce a larger wave.

What you need to remember

wave, energy, amplitude, frequency, wavelength, peak, trough, transverse, longitudinal, close together, further apart, reflection, incident, reflected, superpose

P2.2

A **a** vocal cords **b** speakers **c** foot

B vibrate, sound wave, medium, vacuum, particles

C We see fireworks before we hear them. Explosions give out light and sound at the same time. Light travels much faster than sound.
We can see the Sun, but not hear it. Light can travel through a vacuum. Sound cannot travel through a vacuum; it needs a medium such as air to travel through.
Sound travels fastest in solids. The particles in a solid are very close together. The vibration is passed along more quickly than in a gas.

D steel – 5000 m/s; air – 340 m/s; water – 1500 m/s

What you need to remember

vibrate, particles / molecules, vacuum, solid, quickly, light, medium

P2.3

A harder, more, amplitude, more, bigger

B **a** wave 1
b waves 1 and 2 have similar (or same) loudness
c they have similar (or same) amplitude

C human – **true, false**; bat – **false, true**; dog – **true, true**

What you need to remember

amplitude, frequency, hertz, 20, infrasound, ultrasound, audible, higher

P2.4

A (clockwise from top-left) pinna, ossicles, semi-circular canals, auditory nerve, cochlea, eardrum, auditory canal

B 5, 3, 1, 2, 6, 7, 8, 4
C eardrum, cochlea, auditory nerve
D Listening to very loud music for a long time can cause permanent damage to your hair cells.
A sharp object punching a hole in your eardrum will cause temporary damage until the eardrum grows back.
Listening to loud music for a short time can cause temporary damage until the hair cells have recovered.

What you need to remember

ear, pinna, auditory, eardrum, ossicles, amplify, cochlea, hair, nerve, brain, decibels, damage, diaphragm, electrical, amplifier

P2.5

A sound, frequency, high, 20 000
B Sperm whales hunt in deep water so deep that there is too little light to see. Some dolphins hunt across the seabed to find prey buried out of sight. Bats hunt at night when there is very light to see by.
C 1, 4, 2, 3
D **two** from: sonar to measure depth of seabed below a ship; imaging cancer; treating pain and swelling; measuring size of a room

What you need to remember

ultrasound, 20 000, sonar, transmitter, reflects / echoes, receiver, time, echo, echoes, reverberation

P1 Chapter 2 Pinchpoint

A this is an incorrect answer – both waves **X** and **Y** have a higher amplitude and are therefore louder, but wave **X** does **not** a higher pitch, it has a lower frequency / longer wavelength (fewer waves per second)
B this is an incorrect answer – wave **X** has a lower frequency / longer wavelength (fewer waves per second), therefore **lower** pitch
C this is the correct answer
D this is an incorrect answer – wave **Z** has a higher frequency / shorter wavelength (more waves per second) and therefore a higher pitch; however, **so does wave Y**. In fact the frequency of **Y** and **Z** is the same; only their amplitude differs.

Pinchpoint follow-up

A **a** R   **b** Q
B more complete waves in same time / shorter wavelength / time interval between neighbouring peaks (or troughs) is smaller / more peaks and troughs, more crossings of the horizontal axis in same time / it goes up and down more often in same time (**not** it goes up and down more, or it goes higher)

C
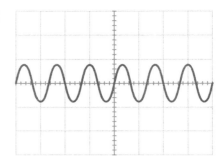

(or similar diagram: higher frequency so more waves, lower amplitude so smaller peak–trough)

D a V
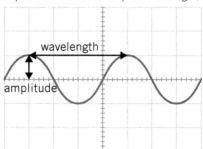

W
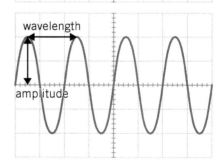

any vertical arrow labelled **amplitude** peak-to-centre, or centre-to-trough; any horizontal arrow same length as shown from peak-to-peak, trough-to-trough, or zero-crossing to similar zero-crossing, labelled **wavelength**
b wave **W**'s wavelength is half wave **V**'s wavelength

P3.1

A source, emits, reflects, absorbed, eye
B 4, 5, 1, 3, 2 (or 1, 3, 4, 5, 2)
C transparent window glass – light is transmitted – you see your friend clearly
opaque bricks of a wall – light is absorbed – you cannot see your friend
translucent frosted window glass – light is scattered – you see your friend, but not clearly
D a 300 000 000 m/s
b 300 000 000 m/s = 300 000 km/s

$$\text{time} = \frac{\text{distance}}{\text{speed}}$$
$$= \frac{250\,000\,000 \text{ km}}{300\,000 \text{ km/s}}$$
$$= 833.3 \text{ s}$$

What you need to remember

luminous, source, non-luminous, reflected, eye, transmit, opaque, translucent, scattered, wave, vacuum, 300 000 000, light-time

P3.2

A behind, upright, laterally inverted, as far behind, virtual, could not, the same

B

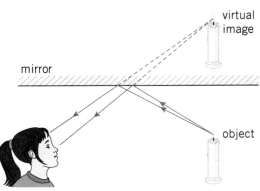

C a angle of reflection = angle of incidence (or both angles are the same / equal)
  b diffuse scattering
  c the light rays striking the surface are parallel; however, because the surface is rough, the angle of incidence is different in different places, so the angle of reflection is different

What you need to remember

reflects, reflects, incident, reflected, normal, equal, incidence, reflection, plane, specular, virtual, diffuse

P3.3

A

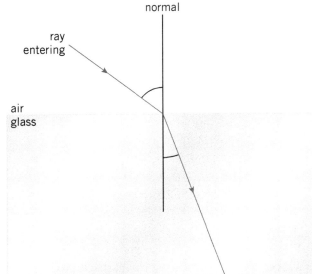

refracted angle should be visibly smaller than incident angle

B light **refracts** when it changes **speed**; light travels **slower** in **glass** than in **air**, so it changes speed as it enters the glass, causing it to **refract** and change **direction**

C

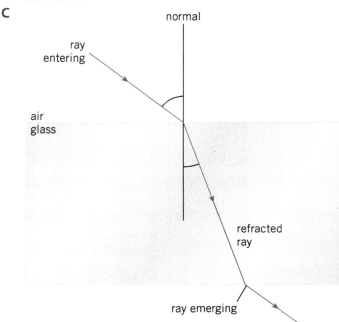

refracted angle inside block should be visibly smaller than incident angle; second refracted angle at bottom of block should be visibly similar to incident angle at the top

D a

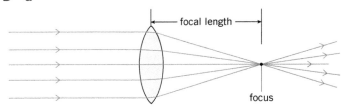

  b refracted, converges, focus / focal point

What you need to remember

medium, speed, direction, refraction, slows down, towards, shallower / less deep, converging, focus

P3.4

A (clockwise from top-left) retina, lens, cornea, pupil, iris, optic nerve

B object – reflected light from this enters the eye; cornea and lens – focus the light; iris – controls the size of the pupil, allowing in more or less light; pupil – a hole that allows light to enter the lens; retina – where the image forms – contains photoreceptors; photoreceptors – rods and cones – absorb light causing a chemical reaction which produces an electrical signal; image – real (you could put a screen here and you would see an image), inverted, smaller than the object; optic nerve – sends electrical signal to the brain

C pinhole, pupil, image, retina

What you need to remember

focusing, object, lens, iris, pupil, retina, photoreceptors, chemical, optic, pixels, pixel, electrical

P3.5

A **a** diagram shows light emerging from right-hand side of prism as a spectrum; colours appear in order, from top: red, orange, yellow, green, blue, indigo, violet; light should be refracted (change direction) at both surfaces, violet is refracted more than red

b different amounts, frequency, most, least

B **a** red, green, blue   **b** yellow

C (labels from left) top: red light, no light; bottom: blue light, no light

D red, black, black, red

What you need to remember

primary, secondary, cyan, primary, white, subtract, subtracts, blue, reflecting, blue, prism, spectrum, dispersion, frequency, lowest, continuous

P1 Chapter 3 Pinchpoint

A this is an incorrect answer – it does **not** show how light reaches your eye. The light reflects off the object (your friend) and into your eye.

B this is an incorrect answer – your friend **does not** emit light. The Sun emits light, which is reflected off your friend and into your eye.

C this is an incorrect answer – your eye **does not** emit light. The Sun emits light, which is reflected off your friend and into your eye.

D this is the correct answer

Pinchpoint follow-up

A one straight line drawn from lamp to anywhere on table with arrowhead pointing from lamp to table; a second straight line drawn from the same spot on the table to anywhere on the eye with arrowhead pointing from table to eye (note: this is diffuse reflection, the table is old and made of wood so has an uneven surface – angles do not have to appear equal in the diagram)

B luminous, non-luminous, reflect, emits, reflected, absorbed

C **a** photoreceptors (or rods and cones)
   b **one** from: chemical reactions / electrical impulse formed / signal sent up the optic nerve to your brain

D **a** from left: object, pinhole, screen
   b photographic film / charge-coupled device (CCD)

P4.1

A **a** the Moon   **b** a comet   **c** Saturn

B Moon, planet, Sun, Solar System, galaxy, Universe

C meteor – rock or dust that burns up as it passes through Earth's atmosphere; Solar System – the Sun and everything that orbits it; galaxy – a collection of billions of stars; star – a natural, luminous object

D GPS satellite for satnav – Earth – artificial
   a moon – a planet – natural
   a planet – Sun – natural
   a comet – Sun – natural
   International Space Station – Earth – artificial

What you need to remember

satellites, orbit, Moon, natural, planets, Mars, Sun, Solar System, comets, stars, galaxy, Milky Way, Universe

P4.2

A comet, meteor, asteroid, planet

B asteroid belt – made up of small rocky bodies, between Mars and Jupiter; Sun – in the centre of the Solar System; a planet – orbits Sun, may be rocky or gas giant; a moon – orbits a planet; a comet – made up of ice and dust; sometimes orbits close to the Sun, sometimes far

C **a** **one** from: all orbit the Sun / all have elliptical orbits / all are round / all orbit in same direction
   b **one** from: rocky planets are smaller (or reverse) / planets nearest to the Sun are smallest (or reverse)
   c **one** from: rocky planets are nearest (or reverse) / smallest planets are nearest (or reverse)

What you need to remember

Solar, Sun, planets, planets, ellipse, Venus, Mars, rock, gas, gases, moons, asteroid, dwarf

P4.3

A **one** from: Sun higher in sky at noon during summer / average temperature higher in summer (or reverse) / days are longer in summer (or reverse) / you see different stars at night

B the Moon – orbits the Earth once a month; the Sun – the Earth spins on its axis once every 24 hours and so different regions of the Earth face the Sun at different times of day; stars – the Earth orbits the Sun once a year and the night-side of the Earth faces different constellations of stars during the year

C **a** the tilt of the Earth's axis means that places in the Northern hemisphere, like London, tilt towards the

Sun in June (summer), so they absorb more of the Sun's rays on a given area of ground, and for longer per day, resulting in higher temperatures; places in the Northern hemisphere tilt away from the Sun in December (winter), so they absorb less of the Sun's rays, and for shorter times per day, resulting in lower temperatures

b in summer, days are longer than in winter; in summer, the northern hemisphere tilts towards the Sun, so the Sun appears to rise above the horizon earlier in the day and set below it later

What you need to remember

day / 24 hours, spins, night, year, orbits, tilt, towards, more, longer, higher

P4.4

A the Sun's light is reflected from the surface of the Moon down to the Earth

B 1 – C; 2 – G; 3 – F; 4 –A; 5 – B; 6 – D; 7 – H; 8 – E

C if the Moon comes between the Sun and the Earth, and completely blocks the light from the Sun reaching the Earth's surface, the Moon casts a shadow on the Earth's surface and this is called a total solar eclipse (or similar: Earth in Moon's shadow; and Sun cannot be seen from that shadow)

What you need to remember

half, Sun, Earth, phases, new, full, month, Sun, Earth, (either order) umbra, solar, penumbra, solar, Moon, lunar

P1 Chapter 4 Pinchpoint

A this is an incorrect answer – the Earth spins on its axis once each **day**. The Sun does not orbit the Earth. It is the Earth that orbits Sun, taking 365 days or 1 **year**.

B this is an incorrect answer – the Earth orbits the Sun once per **year**

C this is an incorrect answer – the Sun and stars do **not** move around us, it is the Earth that orbits the Sun

D this is the correct answer

Pinchpoint follow-up

A

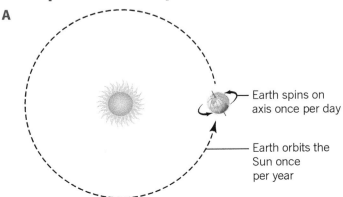

— Earth spins on axis once per day

— Earth orbits the Sun once per year

B spinning, one, orbiting, 365, 365, orbit

C **a** from east to west   **b** axis, year, winter, position

D

Sun

Earth

Moon

area of total eclipse (umbra)   area of partial eclipse (penumbra)

P1 Revision questions

1 newtonmeter [1]

2 pinna [1]; cochlea [1]; ossicles [1]

3 **a** dispersion [1]

  b red, orange, yellow, green, blue, indigo, violet [1]

4 the **Sun emits** light [1]; light **reflects** from the **Moon** [1]

5 days get longer from December to June [1]; days get shorter from June to December [1]

6 two waves in step will add up and produce a bigger wave (larger amplitude) [1]; two waves out of step will produce a smaller wave (smaller amplitude) [1]

7 **a** gravity (or weight) [1]

  b extension is **proportional** to force (or vice versa) (or when force **doubled**, extension **doubles**) [1]

  c 4 cm [1]

8 **two** from: speed [1]; direction [1]; shape [1]

9 **a** when forces are balanced (or similar, e.g. forces cancel out) [1]

  b cup pushes particles of table closer together [1]; bonds between particles are compressed [1]; bonds between particles push back and support cup [1]

  c same type of force [1]; same pair of objects [1]

  d weight = 0.2 kg × 10 N/kg [1]
          = 2 [1] N (or Newtons) [1]

10 **six** from: initially weight is greater than air resistance [1] so forces are unbalanced [1]; skydiver speeds up [1]; when parachute opens, there is a larger surface area [1] and this increases air resistance [1]; air resistance is then greater than the weight [1] so forces are unbalanced [1]; this slows the skydiver down [1]

11 transverse – oscillation (or motion of source or displacement) is at 90° (or right angles or perpendicular or normal) to the direction of the wave [1]; longitudinal – oscillation is parallel to direction of wave (or equivalent terms as above) [1]

12 **a** particles in a liquid are closer together than in a gas [1]; therefore the vibration is passed along more quickly from particle to particle in the liquid than in the gas [1]

b **three** from: sound wave hits diaphragm (flexible plate) [1]; diaphragm vibrates [1]; moves a coil near a magnet [1]; produces an electrical signal [1]

13 a she will see it first [1] because the speed of light is greater than the speed of sound [1]

b temporary [1] or permanent [1] damage to hearing, due to damage to sensitive hair cells in cochlea

14 a **three** from: meteor emits light as it heats up in the atmosphere [1]; light is transmitted through the atmosphere [1]; camera shutter opens, allowing light through [1]; light focused (or refracts) as it passes through lens [1]; light is absorbed at CCD (charge-coupled device) [1]; CCD creates electrical signal which is converted to light on phone screen [1]

b 300 000 000 m/s [1]

15 a add (or mix) green [1] and blue [1]

b red – no [1]; green – yes – green [1]; blue – no [1]

16 the Earth is spinning on its axis (or rotating, throughout) [1]; the Moon and stars moved (almost) the same amount in Figure 3 (or in one hour) due to rotation of Earth [1]; stars are back to (almost) same position in Figure 4 (or in one day) because the Earth takes one day to spin [1]; the Moon has shifted position compared to the stars in Figure 4 (or in one day) because the Moon is orbiting the Earth [1]

17 **two** from: Mars mostly made of rock, Neptune mostly made of gas [1]; Mars hotter and Neptune colder [1]; Mars smaller diameter, Neptune larger diameter [1]

Periodic table

key

relative atomic mass	
atomic symbol	
name	
atomic (proton) number	

1	2											3	4	5	6	7	0
							1 **H** hydrogen 1										4 **He** helium 2
7 **Li** lithium 3	9 **Be** beryllium 4											11 **B** boron 5	12 **C** carbon 6	14 **N** nitrogen 7	16 **O** oxygen 8	19 **F** fluorine 9	20 **Ne** neon 10
23 **Na** sodium 11	24 **Mg** magnesium 12											27 **Al** aluminium 13	28 **Si** silicon 14	31 **P** phosphorus 15	32 **S** sulfur 16	35.5 **Cl** chlorine 17	40 **Ar** argon 18
39 **K** potassium 19	40 **Ca** calcium 20	45 **Sc** scandium 21	48 **Ti** titanium 22	51 **V** vanadium 23	52 **Cr** chromium 24	55 **Mn** manganese 25	56 **Fe** iron 26	59 **Co** cobalt 27	59 **Ni** nickel 28	63.5 **Cu** copper 29	65 **Zn** zinc 30	70 **Ga** gallium 31	73 **Ge** germanium 32	75 **As** arsenic 33	79 **Se** selenium 34	80 **Br** bromine 35	84 **Kr** krypton 36
85 **Rb** rubidium 37	88 **Sr** strontium 38	89 **Y** yttrium 39	91 **Zr** zirconium 40	93 **Nb** niobium 41	96 **Mo** molybdenum 42	[98] **Tc** technetium 43	101 **Ru** ruthenium 44	103 **Rh** rhodium 45	106 **Pd** palladium 46	108 **Ag** silver 47	112 **Cd** cadmium 48	115 **In** indium 49	119 **Sn** tin 50	122 **Sb** antimony 51	128 **Te** tellurium 52	127 **I** iodine 53	131 **Xe** xenon 54
133 **Cs** caesium 55	137 **Ba** barium 56	139 **La*** lanthanum 57	178 **Hf** hafnium 72	181 **Ta** tantalum 73	184 **W** tungsten 74	186 **Re** rhenium 75	190 **Os** osmium 76	192 **Ir** iridium 77	195 **Pt** platinum 78	197 **Au** gold 79	201 **Hg** mercury 80	204 **Tl** thallium 81	207 **Pb** lead 82	209 **Bi** bismuth 83	[209] **Po** polonium 84	[210] **At** astatine 85	[222] **Rn** radon 86
[223] **Fr** francium 87	[226] **Ra** radium 88	[227] **Ac*** actinium 89	[261] **Rf** rutherfordium 104	[262] **Db** dubnium 105	[266] **Sg** seaborgium 106	[264] **Bh** bohrium 107	[277] **Hs** hassium 108	[268] **Mt** meitnerium 109	[271] **Ds** darmstadtium 110	[272] **Rg** roentgenium 111	[285] **Cn** copernicium 112	[286] **Nh** nihonium 113	[289] **Fl** flerovium 114	[289] **Mc** moscovium 115	[293] **Lv** livermorium 116	[294] **Ts** tennessine 117	[294] **Og** oganesson 118

*The lanthanides (atomic numbers 58–71) and the actinides (atomic numbers 90–103) have been omitted.

Great Clarendon Street, Oxford, OX2 6DP, United Kingdom

Oxford University Press is a department of the University of Oxford.
It furthers the University's objective of excellence in research,
scholarship, and education by publishing worldwide. Oxford is a
registered trade mark of Oxford University Press in the UK and in
certain other countries

British Library Cataloguing in Publication Data
Data available

978-1-38-203009-0

10 9 8 7 6

Paper used in the production of this book is a natural, recyclable
product made from wood grown in sustainable forests.
The manufacturing process conforms to the environmental regulations
of the country of origin.

Printed and bound by CPI Group (UK) Ltd, Croydon, CR0 4YY

Acknowledgements

The publisher and the authors would like to thank the following for
permission to use their photographs:

Cover image: Sebastian Tomus/Shutterstock; **p101**: David Parker/
Science Photo Library
p96(L): pockygallery/Shutterstock; **p96**(M): solarseven/Shutterstock;
p96(R): Shutterstock

All artwork by Aptara